T0326824

ON THEOLOGICAL
INTERPRETATION

ON THEOLOGICAL INTERPRETATION

Scott R. Swain

The Trinity and the Bible: On Theological Interpretation

Lexham Academic, an imprint of Lexham Press
1313 Commercial St., Bellingham, WA 98225
LexhamPress.com

Print ISBN 9781683595359
Digital ISBN 9781683595366
Library of Congress Control Number 2021935523

Lexham Editorial: Todd Hains, Jeff Reimer, Abigail Salinger, Mandi Newell
Cover Design: Joshua Hunt, Brittany Schrock
Typesetting: Justin Marr

For my Doktorvater,
Kevin J. Vanhoozer

CONTENTS

Abbreviations xi

Prayer to the Holy Trinity xiii

1 (Re)turning to the Subject 1
The Trinity and Biblical Interpretation

2 The Bible and the Trinity in Recent Thought 7
Review, Analysis, and Constructive Proposal

3 B. B. Warfield and the Biblical Doctrine of the Trinity 31
A Historical Experiment

4 God's Lordly Son 59
Mark 12:35–37 and Trinitarian Christology

5 Heirs through God 83
Galatians 4:4–7 and the Doctrine of the Trinity

6 To Him Who Sits on the Throne and to the Lamb 97
Hymning God's Triune Name in Revelation 4–5

7 Seven Axioms 121
On the Trinity, the Bible, and Theological Interpretation

ABBREVIATIONS

A(Y)B	Anchor (Yale) Bible
IJST	*International Journal of Systematic Theology*
JBL	*Journal of Biblical Literature*
JSNT	*Journal for the Study of the New Testament*
LXX	Septuagint
NIGTC	New International Greek Testament Commentary
NTS	*New Testament Studies*
SIET	Strategic Initiatives in Evangelical Theology
WBC	Word Biblical Commentary
WUNT	Wissenschaftliche Untersuchungen zum Neuen Testament

PRAYER TO THE HOLY TRINITY

In the name of the Father and of the Son and of the Holy Spirit. Amen.

Holy, holy, holy is the LORD of hosts. *Isa 6:3*
From him and through him and to him are all things. *Rom 11:36*
Ascribe to the LORD the glory due his name;
worship the LORD in the splendor of holiness.
The voice of the LORD is over the waters;
the God of glory thunders, the LORD, over many waters.
The voice of the LORD is powerful;
the voice of the LORD is full of majesty. *Ps 29:2–4*

Glory be to the Father and to the Son and to the Holy Spirit,
as it was in the beginning, is now, and will be forever. Amen.

Almighty and everlasting God, You have given us, Your servants, grace to acknowledge the glory of the eternal Trinity by the confession of a true faith and to worship the Unity in the power of the Divine Majesty. Keep us steadfast in this faith and defend us always from all adversities; who lives and reigns, one God—Father, Son, and Holy Spirit—now and forever. Amen.

(RE)TURNING TO THE SUBJECT

THE TRINITY AND BIBLICAL INTERPRETATION

The essays that follow have a common focus: the Triune God who presents himself to us in holy Scripture as the object of our shared knowledge, love, and praise. Though some consideration is given to the manner in which the Trinity reveals himself in the prophetic and apostolic writings and also to the ways in which the church has received that revelation in its confession and theology, the primary focus of these essays is exegesis: the act of loving attention we give to the historical and literary shape of scriptural texts in order to discern the singular identity and activity of the Triune God who presents himself therein (Deut 4:32–40; 6:4; 1 Cor 8:6; Eph 4:4–6).

The arguments made in this volume would be hard to conceive apart from the broader retrieval of Trinitarian biblical exegesis we have witnessed over the past several decades. The recovery of the Trinity as the subject matter of exegetical attention is downstream from an earlier recovery of the Trinity as the subject matter of dogmatic attention. That recovery led to the production of significant theological and historical treatments of the doctrine. Among the latter, studies of various church fathers (set within the context of an emerging pro-Nicene culture), medieval doctors, and Protestant divines have enriched our understanding of the history of biblical interpretation and theology. More recently the flourishing of Trinitarian theology can be traced to studies devoted to what Karl Barth once called the "root" of Trinitarian doctrine—biblical exegesis.

From the standpoint of academic theology, the rise of renewed interest in Trinitarian biblical exegesis is nearly miraculous. Once regarded as the later Hellenistic corruption of primitive evangelical religion, far removed from the minds of Jesus, the apostolic church, and its Scriptures, the Trinity has been restored to its rightful place as an object of interpretive attention through the work of biblical scholars and theologians such as Michael Allen, Matthew Bates, Mark Gignilliat, Wesley Hill, Bobby Jamieson, Robert Jenson, Madison Pierce, Kavin Rowe, Fred Sanders, Andrea Saner, Christopher Seitz, Katherine Sonderegger, Kendall Soulen, Kevin Vanhoozer, Francis Watson, and David Yeago, along with many others.

These scholars have helped facilitate the recovery of Trinitarian biblical exegesis from what, hermeneutically speaking, may be likened to the condition of those who have suffered certain brain injuries. In such conditions, patients retain their ability to recognize features (for example, eyes, noses, mouths) but not faces.[1] This hermeneutical condition not only afflicts more atomistic approaches to biblical exegesis. It also afflicts certain heirs of J. P. Gabler's approach to biblical theology. The latter often enough address questions about the deity of Jesus—a vital topic for Trinitarian theology! However, due to specific habits inherited from historical biblical criticism, they tend to do so without benefit of categories and interpretive practices within which such questions make good historical and theological sense.

Recent approaches to Trinitarian biblical exegesis have facilitated recovery from this lamentable hermeneutical condition

1. See Rowan Williams, *Being Human: Bodies, Minds, Persons* (Grand Rapids: Eerdmans, 2018), 54.

by reconnecting the New Testament christological teaching to Old Testament monotheism; through deeper awareness of the historical, religious, and philosophical contexts within which the writings of Second Temple Judaism and the New Testament emerged; through careful reception-historical attention to historical and theological categories and practices of biblical interpretation (for example, relations, prosopological exegesis, partitive exegesis), along with confidence in Scripture's status as prophetic and apostolic witness to the appearance and action of the Triune God in history. The result, hermeneutically speaking, is a better capacity for perceiving the primary ascriptive subject of holy Scripture, the Triune God.

The studies that follow were produced over the course of the past decade. Some of them began as formal academic lectures; all of them have been published previously in various books and journals. The first and second chapters address the broader hermeneutical framework of Trinitarian biblical exegesis as well as the reception of one particular instance of such exegesis in North American Reformed and evangelical theology. The final three chapters address different aspects of Trinitarian theology by means of exegetical attention to different forms of New Testament literature, including Gospel, Epistle, and apocalyptic.

The essays were not originally written with a larger work in view. Despite their differences in relative degree of exegetical rigor and intended audience, they nevertheless share a number of common features: interest in ontological (as opposed to merely ethical or soteriological) dimensions of biblical monotheism, the conviction that "relation" provides the most meaningful category for identifying the persons of the Trinity, impatience with the modern divide (sometimes exacerbated by proponents of theological interpretation of Scripture) between historical biblical criticism and the history of biblical interpretation, and dissatisfaction with modern ways of distinguishing immanent and economic Trinity.

I have incurred many debts in the process of producing these essays. I am grateful to Mark Elliott for the opportunity to participate in the Galatians and Christian Theology conference at the University of St. Andrews in 2012. Thanks also are due to Sam Storms for inviting me to deliver a plenary address at the annual meeting of the Evangelical Theological Society in 2016. Christina Mansfield and Tyler Freire assisted me in bringing the present volume to publication.

Over the past twenty-two years my *Doktorvater* Kevin Vanhoozer has been an academic mentor, a sounding board and an encourager in various facets of my personal and professional life, and a friend. In gratitude for his friendship, and in honor of his sixty-fifth birthday, I dedicate this collection of essays to him.

THE BIBLE AND THE TRINITY IN RECENT THOUGHT

REVIEW, ANALYSIS, AND CONSTRUCTIVE PROPOSAL

For us there is one God, the Father, from whom are all things and for whom we exist, and one Lord, Jesus Christ, through whom are all things and through whom we exist.

1 *Corinthians 8:6*

Christians confess the holy Trinity. "For us there is one God, the Father, from whom are all things and for whom we exist, and one Lord, Jesus Christ, through whom are all things and through whom we exist" (1 Cor 8:6). Christians confess the holy Trinity on the basis of holy Scripture. The Bible proclaims a Triune Creator (Ps 33:6; John 1:1–3) and a Triune Redeemer (Gal 4:4–6). The Bible, moreover, promises a Triune reward to its faithful readers: "The river of the water of life ... flowing from the throne of God and of the Lamb" (Rev 22:1) is our promised inheritance (Rev 21:6–7). Holy Scripture mandates baptism in God's Triune name (Matt 28:19), calls us to bless God's Triune name (Eph 1:3–14), and blesses us in God's Triune name: "The grace of the Lord Jesus Christ and the love of God and the fellowship of the Holy Spirit be with you all" (2 Cor 13:14). The Trinity is the foundation of typological reasoning: God's agency through

Christ and the Spirit connects Israel's exodus and Christian baptism because in both events both parties "drink of one Spirit" (1 Cor 12:13; see also 10:1–4). And the Trinity is the foundation of moral reasoning: Paul urges the Ephesians to "maintain the unity of the Spirit in the bond of peace" (Eph 4:3) because "there is one body and one Spirit ... one Lord, one faith, one baptism, one God and Father of all, who is over all and through all and in all" (Eph 4:4–6). The unified testimony of holy Scripture is that all things are from and through and to the Triune God (1 Cor 8:6). "To him be glory forever" (Rom 11:36).

Christian theology's interest in the relationship between the Bible and the Trinity follows from their mutual implication within the Christian confession. When Christian theology directs its attention to the relationship between the Bible and the Trinity, it confronts a number of important questions. There is the fundamental question of *whether* the Trinity is actually in the Bible, a question disputed since the rise of modern biblical criticism that remains with us today. There is also the question of *what* kind of Trinity is in the Bible. Recent evangelical controversy surrounding the Trinity reveals that agreement on the former question does not guarantee agreement on the latter question.[1] There is, finally, the question of *how* the Trinity is in the Bible. How does the Triune God teach us to confess his holy name in and through the writings of holy Scripture? Addressing the "how" question, I suggest, best prepares us to address the "whether" and the "what" questions. Indeed, the controversy of recent days indicates that missteps regarding the question of what kind of Trinity is in the

---

1. Consider, for example, the debate that erupted in 2016 regarding eternal relations of authority and submission within the Trinity. For a recent defense of eternal relations of authority and submission, see Bruce A. Ware and John Starke, ed., *One God in Three Persons: Unity of Essence, Distinction of Persons, Implications for Life* (Wheaton: Crossway, 2015). For a critique, see Michael F. Bird and Scott Harrower, ed., *Trinity Without Hierarchy: Reclaiming Nicene Orthodoxy in Trinitarian Theology* (Grand Rapids: Kregel, 2019).

Bible are intrinsically connected to missteps regarding the question of how the Trinity is in the Bible.

I want to focus on the question of how the Trinity is in the Bible by taking a tour of some of the most significant recent studies on the Bible and the Trinity. Along the way, I will chart a constructive pathway for analyzing the Bible's Trinitarian discourse. Our tour will proceed in two broad movements. First, I will engage in methodological ground clearing. Second, I will discuss three patterns of divine naming that indicate how the Trinity is in the Bible, each of which is found in 1 Corinthians 8:6, our lodestar for this essay. In 1 Corinthians 8:6, as well as in a host of other biblical texts, we see a *monotheistic pattern* of divine naming, a *relational pattern* of divine naming, and a *metaphysical pattern* of divine naming. Taken together, these patterns reveal how the Trinity is in the Bible. In learning to recognize and read these patterns rightly, Trinitarian theology may better learn to follow the Word as it leads us into the knowledge and love of the Triune God.

THE BIBLE IN THE TRINITY

We cannot fully appreciate how "the Trinity is in the Bible" without observing how "the Bible is in the Trinity."[2] While the Bible is the cognitive principle of the Trinity, the supreme source from which our knowledge of the Trinity is drawn, the Trinity is the ontological principle of the Bible. The Trinity is not simply one of the things about which the Bible speaks. The Trinity is the speaker from whom the Bible and all things proceed: "For us there is one God, the Father, from whom are all things ... and one Lord, Jesus Christ, through whom are all things" (1 Cor 8:6). All things in heaven and on earth, including holy Scripture, are

2. Fred Sanders, *The Triune God*, New Studies in Dogmatics (Grand Rapids: Zondervan Academic, 2016), 44, 88–91.

"produced by the creative breath of the Almighty"[3] (See Ps 33:6; 2 Tim 3:16).

Recent work on Scripture and hermeneutics rightly locates the Bible and its interpretation within a Trinitarian economy of revelation.[4] According to the late John Webster, "a prudent theology will treat questions concerning the nature and interpretation of Scripture ... as corollaries of more primary theological teaching about the relation of God and creatures."[5] Adopting this approach leads us to see "Holy Scripture and its interpretation" as "elements in the domain of the Word of God," a domain whose source and scope are Trinitarian in nature. "In fulfilment of the eternal purpose of God the Father (Eph. 1.9, 11), and by sending the Spirit of wisdom and revelation (Eph. 1.17), the Son sheds abroad the knowledge of himself and of all things in himself."[6] Kevin Vanhoozer and Dan Treier agree. Viewing the Bible within the domain of the Word enables us to perceive its *nature* as "a text that is authored (ultimately) by God, with God (Jesus Christ) as its ultimate content, and with God (Holy Spirit) as its ultimate interpreter."[7] Viewing the Bible within the domain of the Word also enables us to perceive its *purpose* as "part of a divinely administered economy of light by which the triune God establishes and

---

3. B. B. Warfield, *The Inspiration and Authority of the Bible* (Phillipsburg, NJ: Presbyterian & Reformed, 1948), 296.

4. Representative works include Matthew Levering, *Participatory Biblical Exegesis: A Theology of Biblical Interpretation* (Notre Dame: University of Notre Dame Press, 2008); Stephen E. Fowl, *Theological Interpretation of Scripture*, Cascade Companions (Eugene, OR: Cascade, 2009); J. Todd Billings, *The Word of God for the People of God: An Entryway to the Theological Interpretation of Scripture* (Grand Rapids: Eerdmans, 2010); Scott R. Swain, *Trinity, Revelation, and Reading: A Theological Introduction to the Bible and its Interpretation* (London: T&T Clark, 2011); John Webster, *The Domain of the Word: Scripture and Theological Reason* (London: T&T Clark, 2012); Kevin J. Vanhoozer and Daniel J. Treier, *Theology and the Mirror of Scripture: A Mere Evangelical Account*, Studies in Christian Doctrine and Scripture (Downers Grove, IL: IVP Academic, 2015).

5. Webster, *Domain of the Word*, 3.

6. Webster, *Domain of the Word*, 3.

7. Vanhoozer and Treier, *Theology and the Mirror of Scripture*, 73.

administers covenantal relations with its readers."[8] "Scripture is a means of God's self-presentation."[9]

Fred Sanders's book *The Triune God* demonstrates the hermeneutical payoff of adopting this standpoint. Sanders draws on G. K. Beale and Benjamin Gladd's work on the biblical theology of "mystery" to anchor his understanding of the Trinitarian economy of revelation.[10] Attending to the mysterious shape of biblical revelation, he argues that "the Trinity is ... a mystery in the New Testament sense of the term: something always true, long concealed, and now revealed."[11] More specifically, the full revelation of the Triune God comes by means of the personal presence of the Son and the Spirit in their respective missions: "In order to inform us that the Father has a Son and a Holy Spirit, the Father sent the Son and the Holy Spirit in person."[12] The Old Testament adumbrates this revelation of the Trinity, "shadowing forth" the revelation of the Trinity *before* the Son and the Spirit appeared in person to save and to sanctify us, while the New Testament attests it, bearing witness to the revelation of the Trinity *after* those saving and sanctifying appearances.[13] Sanders's work not only opens up promising possibilities for responsible Trinitarian exegesis of the Old and New Testaments but also offers an intriguing account of the unity of the Old and New Testaments. For Sanders, the Trinitarian economy of salvation "binds the two

8. Vanhoozer and Treier, *Theology and the Mirror of Scripture*, 74.

9. Vanhoozer and Treier, *Theology and the Mirror of Scripture*, 75. The contemporary emphasis on Scripture's status as the word of the Triune God that ministers the presence of the Triune God is not without precedent among an earlier generation of evangelical theologians. J. I. Packer describes the Bible as "God the Father preaching God the Son in the power of God the Holy Spirit" (*God Has Spoken: Revelation and the Bible*, 3rd ed. [Grand Rapids: Baker, 1998], 91).

10. G. K. Beale and Benjamin L. Gladd, *Hidden but Now Revealed: A Biblical Theology of Mystery* (Downers Grove, IL: IVP Academic, 2014).

11. Sanders, *Triune God*, 37.

12. Sanders, *Triune God*, 40.

13. Sanders, *Triune God*, chapters 7–8.

testaments together as one canon … whose center of attention is the *oikonomia* (Eph 1:10) but whose horizon includes the eternal being of God above history."[14]

THE MODE OF THE TRINITY'S PRESENCE IN THE BIBLE

The Bible is the product of the Triune God through which he (mysteriously) adumbrates and attests his self-presentation to his people. This, in part, is what it means to affirm that the Bible is in the Trinity. Turning toward our focal question about how the Trinity is in the Bible requires that we attend more closely to the mode of God's self-presentation in holy Scripture.

The Trinity does not present himself to us in holy Scripture in the specific words of the Nicene-Constantinopolitan Creed. Some, of course, claim this as evidence that the Trinity does not present himself to us in any form in the Bible and that the church's Trinitarian dogma is the product of later, extrabiblical influences on its thinking, life, and liturgy. Wilhelm Bousset argued that it was only when the church had forgotten its Jewish monotheistic roots that it could, under the influences of its Hellenistic context, affirm the deity of Jesus Christ.[15] The church's Trinitarian dogma, according to this view, is "a work of the Greek Spirit on the soil of the Gospel," to use Adolf von Harnack's famous description.[16] Martin Hengel and others have undermined Bousset's sharp distinction between an early Palestinian form of Christianity and a later Hellenized form.[17] Richard Bauckham and Larry Hurtado, representatives of what Hengel dubbed the "new history of

---

14. Sanders, *Triune God*, 45.

15. Wilhelm Bousset, *Kyrios Christos*, trans. John E. Steely (Nashville: Abingdon, 1970).

16. Adolf von Harnack, *History of Dogma*, trans. Neil Buchanan (Boston: Little, Brown, & Co., 1905), 1:17.

17. Martin Hengel, *Judaism and Hellenism: Studies in Their Encounter in Palestine During the Early Hellenistic Period*, trans. John Bowden (Philadelphia: Fortress, 1981).

religions school," have further discredited Bousset's theory, demonstrating that the early church identified Jesus *with* and worshiped Jesus *as* the one true God of Israel.[18] The suggestion that Greek philosophical influences drove the church to a Trinitarian confession is, at any rate, highly implausible. As Mark Edwards observes, "The paradoxical notion of three persons, each identical with the one God but none identical with the other two, is one that no philosopher would have permitted to ensnare him if he were entirely free to choose his own premises."[19] Something else must have pressed the church to confess a Triune God.

The church confesses the Trinity on the basis of holy Scripture. If we admit, though, that the Trinity does not present himself to us in the Bible in creedal form, where does that leave us? And what is the relationship between the biblical form of God's Triune self-presentation and the creedal form of the church's Trinitarian confession?[20]

Recent studies suggest different ways of thinking about the presence of the Trinity in the Bible. According to Ben Witherington and Laura Ice, the New Testament provides "raw data" that the church later synthesizes in the form of a "developed doctrine of the Trinity."[21] Matthew Levering appeals to Witherington and Ice's metaphor to describe the Trinitarian theology of Thomas Aquinas. According to Levering, "Aquinas draws upon the 'developed doctrine' as elaborated by the Fathers and

---

18. Larry Hurtado, *One God, One Lord: Early Christian Devotion and Ancient Jewish Monotheism* (Philadelphia: Fortress, 1988); Richard Bauckham, *Jesus and the God of Israel: God Crucified and Other Studies on the New Testament's Christology of Divine Identity* (Grand Rapids: Eerdmans, 2009).

19. Mark Edwards, "Exegesis and the Early Christian Doctrine of the Trinity," in *The Oxford Handbook of the Trinity*, ed. Gilles Emery and Matthew Levering (Oxford: Oxford University Press, 2011), 80.

20. For an intriguing treatment of the latter question, see Craig A. Blaising, "Creedal Formation as Hermeneutical Development: A Reexamination of Nicaea," *Pro Ecclesia* 19 (2010): 371–88.

21. Ben Witherington III and Laura Ice, *The Shadow of the Almighty: Father, Son, and Spirit in Biblical Perspective* (Grand Rapids: Eerdmans, 2002), xi.

by his medieval predecessors, and as enunciated by the Church's creedal formulations" and "sapientially illumines" the raw data of "the New Testament's revelation of the Trinity ... with contemplative clarity that, by purifying our knowing, crystallizes (as it were) the steps of the mystical dance revealed in Christ who, through the Spirit, invites our participation in the inexhaustible life of the Father."[22] Employing a slightly different idiom, Gordon Fee describes Paul as a "latent trinitarian," whose experience of God through Christ and the Spirit affords him "new and expanded ways of talking about God as Saviour—while at the same time rigorously maintaining his monotheism."[23] The Trinity is in the New Testament, according to Fee, not as fully developed doctrine, but as "experienced reality."[24] While Fee agrees that Paul's experience of the Trinity informs later creedal statements of the doctrine, he warns us not to "spend our labors on the ontological questions in such a way as to lose the essential narrative about God and salvation that raised those questions in the first place."[25] According to Witherington and Ice, Levering, and Fee, then, the Trinity is in the Bible in an *undeveloped form*. On this construal, the task of Trinitarian theology in relation to the Bible is to develop what is undeveloped without destroying the natural narrative habitat that generated the undeveloped form of the doctrine in the first place.

In a short essay devoted to Paul's teaching about God in Romans and Galatians, Richard Hays suggests an alternative construal of the presence of the Trinity in the Bible. While Hays acknowledges that Paul "did not know the doctrinal formulae

---

22. Matthew Levering, *Scripture and Metaphysics: Aquinas and the Renewal of Trinitarian Theology*, Challenges in Contemporary Theology (Oxford: Blackwell, 2004), 196.

23. Gordon D. Fee, "Paul and the Trinity: The Experience of Christ and the Spirit for Paul's Understanding of God," in *The Trinity: An Interdisciplinary Symposium on the Trinity*, ed. Stephen T. Davis, Daniel Kendall, and Gerald O'Collins (Oxford: Oxford University Press, 1999), 51.

24. Fee, "Paul and the Trinity," 49.

25. Fee, "Paul and the Trinity," 72.

worked out in the fourth-century church's theological reflection about the one God in three persons," he argues that Paul's "prayers, praises, and narratives about ... God point to the same complex reality with which the ecumenical councils later grappled."[26] The relationship between the mode of the Trinity's presence in the Bible and the mode of the Trinity's presence in the creeds is not, according to Hays, a relationship between raw data and developed doctrine. Drawing on the work of Frances Young and David Ford, Hays argues that the relationship between the Trinity in the Bible and the Trinity in the creeds is similar to the relationship between the fluent speaker of a language and the theoretical grammar of that language. As Hays explains, "A person does not need to know theoretical grammar constructs in order to speak grammatically. In fact, it is the reverse: 'Grammar' is developed to explain the linguistic practices of those who speak a complex language with unreflective fluency. In the same way, the later doctrine of the Trinity is an attempt to describe and analyze the way in which Jesus Christ and the Spirit had 'become intrinsic to Paul's way of referring to God.'"[27]

Hays's metaphor correlates well with Oswald Bayer's conception of theology as a "grammar of the language of Holy Scripture."[28] Trinitarian *theology*, according to this conception, is commentary on and reflective analysis of the primary and normatively fluent Trinitarian *language* of holy Scripture. As we will see more fully below, what we have in the Bible is not merely an experience of the Trinity or the as yet undeveloped raw data of Trinitarian reflection. What we have in the Bible is well-formed Trinitarian

---

26. Richard B. Hays, "The God of Mercy Who Rescues Us from the Present Evil Age," in *The Forgotten God: Perspectives in Biblical Theology*, ed. A. Andrew Das and Frank J. Matera (Louisville: Westminster John Knox, 2002), 141.

27. Hays, "God of Mercy," 141.

28. Bayer draws this phrase from Hamann who, in turn, is dependent on Luther. See Oswald Bayer, *Theology the Lutheran Way*, ed. and trans. Jeffrey G. Silcock and Mark C. Mattes (Grand Rapids: Eerdmans, 2007), 81, 94–96, 125–26, 170.

discourse: primary, normative, fluent. More specifically, we have the Triune God's self-naming in the form of the Spirit-inspired prophetic and apostolic testimony to that self-naming. The Trinitarian theology of the church's creeds, proclamation, and liturgy, therefore, is not a refinement of or an improvement on God's self-naming in Scripture. It is rather the church's attempt, in prayerful thought and speech, to follow the divine Word as it leads us out of the misery of idolatry into the happiness that lies before us in the vision of the Triune God.

ON DIVINE NAMING

The divine name is the primary mode of God's self-presentation in holy Scripture. The Christian doctrine of the Trinity is the interpretation of the Bible's Triune naming for the instruction, conversion, consolation, and direction of the church in its pilgrimage toward the place where the Triune God will no longer address us in holy Scripture but rather face-to-face.[29]

The foundational act of divine naming that the Bible adumbrates and attests is not the creature's naming of God, but God's naming of himself.[30] God sanctifies and commissions prophets and apostles to be ministers of his Word by naming himself in their presence. At the burning bush, YHWH expounds his name to Moses, "I AM WHO I AM" (Exod 3:14). Again at Mount Sinai, God reveals his glory to Moses by proclaiming his name, "YHWH, YHWH, a God merciful and gracious, slow to anger, and

29. Khaled Anatolios states, "The task of trinitarian theology is not to claim fully adequate expressions or analyses of divine being but to clarify the rules generated by God's self-revelation that enable us to successfully refer our being and activity, knowingly and lovingly, to Father, Son, and Holy Spirit" (*Retrieving Nicaea: The Development and Meaning of Trinitarian Doctrine* [Grand Rapids: Baker Academic, 2011], 292).

30. William Desmond, *God and the Between* (Oxford: Blackwell, 2008), 281. Contrast this with modern mediating theology's attempt to ground the Trinity in either history or experience (Samuel M. Powell, *The Trinity in German Thought* [Cambridge: Cambridge University Press, 2001]).

abounding in steadfast love and faithfulness" (Exod 34:6).[31] In similar fashion, on the Mount of Transfiguration Peter, James, and John are set apart for their apostolic ministry, becoming eyewitnesses of God's glory as they become "ear-witnesses"—to borrow Vanhoozer's happy term—of an intra-Trinitarian event of divine self-naming: "This is my beloved Son, with whom I am well pleased" (Matt 17:5; 2 Pet 1:16–18; John 1:14).[32] The foundation of the prophetic and apostolic witness, and thus of the prophetic and apostolic writings, is the self-naming of the Triune God.

While divine self-naming is the *foundational* form of divine naming that we witness in holy Scripture, it is not the *only* form of divine naming that we witness in holy Scripture. By naming himself in the presence of prophets, God sets them apart to "proclaim the name of the LORD" (Deut 32:3). The proclamation of God's holy name by God's holy prophets in turn awakens the entire congregation of God's creatures to call on the name of the Lord: "My mouth will speak the praise of the LORD, and let all flesh bless his holy name forever and ever" (Ps 145:21). In similar fashion, God's triune self-naming at Jesus' baptism (Matt 3:16–17) leads, through the ministry of the apostles, to the foundation of a community that baptizes "in the name of the Father and of the Son and of the Holy Spirit" (Matt 28:19; 1 John 1:1–3). The foundational revelatory act of divine self-naming thus endows a community of divine naming.[33]

The various additional forms of divine naming that compose the community of divine naming that is the prophetic and apostolic writings are no less the Word of God than God's foundational

---

31. According to Mark Gignilliat, "YHWH's proclamation of his own name *is* the revelation of his glory" (Gignilliat, "The Trinity and the Old Testament: Real Presence or Imposition?," in *The Essential Trinity: New Testament Foundations and Practical Relevance*, ed. Brandon D. Crowe and Carl R. Trueman [London: Apollos, 2016], 181).

32. Kevin J. Vanhoozer, *Remythologizing Theology: Divine Action, Passion, and Authorship*, Cambridge Studies in Christian Doctrine (Cambridge: Cambridge University Press, 2010), 1.

33. Desmond, *God and the Between*, 281.

acts of self-naming.[34] If the hermeneutical task of Trinitarian theology is the interpretation of the divine names, then that task must include analyzing the patterns that various biblical forms of divine naming adumbrate and attest.

THREE PATTERNS OF DIVINE NAMING

First Corinthians 8:6 plays a central role in recent debates regarding the nature of monotheism and Christology in the New Testament writings. Paul's self-involving confession regarding the identity and activity of God and Christ is relevant to the present discussion insofar as it illustrates three patterns of divine naming that recur in various forms across various biblical texts.

A MONOTHEISTIC PATTERN OF DIVINE NAMING

> For us there is one God ... and one Lord. (1 Cor 8:6)

The first pattern of divine naming that 1 Corinthians 8:6 attests is a monotheistic pattern of divine naming. In this pattern of divine naming, the primary Trinitarian language of the Bible *identifies* God, Jesus, and the Spirit *with* YHWH the one true God of Israel. First Corinthians 8:6 offers an example of this pattern in its application of Deuteronomy 6:4 to God and Christ.[35] Much of the literature relevant to our topic in recent years demonstrates the various ways the New Testament exhibits a monotheistic pattern of divine naming.

Larry Hurtado's several works on this subject detect the presence of both an "exclusivist monotheism" and "an inclusion of

---

34. Henri Blocher's recent treatment of inspiration is relevant here: "God and the Scripture Writers: The Question of Double Authorship," in *The Enduring Authority of the Christian Scriptures*, ed. D. A. Carson (Grand Rapids: Eerdmans, 2016), especially 531.

35. Summaries of recent discussions may be found in Anthony C. Thiselton, *The First Epistle to the Corinthians: A Commentary on the Greek Text*, NIGTC (Grand Rapids: Eerdmans, 2000), 631–38; and N. T. Wright, *Paul and the Faithfulness of God*, vol. 2, parts 3 and 4 (Minneapolis: Fortress, 2013), 634–56, 661–70.

Christ along with God as rightful recipient of cultic devotion" within the New Testament.[36] Richard Bauckham demonstrates how early Christian writings include Jesus within the identity of the one God by applying to Jesus not only the unique divine name but also the unique identifying descriptions of Jewish creational and eschatological monotheism.[37] Chris Tilling and N. T. Wright reveal further texture in this pattern of divine naming by demonstrating how Old Testament language of God's unique covenant relationship to Israel and of God's promised return to Zion are applied to Jesus by New Testament authors.[38] In his book *The Divine Name(s) and the Holy Trinity*, the first of a promised two volumes on this topic, Kendall Soulen traces the extent and manner in which the New Testament applies the Tetragrammaton, by means of its Greek surrogate *kyrios* as well as its radiant "corona of connotation," to the Father, the Son, and the Spirit.[39] The detailed exegetical analyses of Kavin Rowe, Gordon Fee, and Richard Hays further confirm the ubiquity of this monotheistic pattern of divine naming in holy Scripture.[40]

Although this monotheistic pattern of divine naming has not gained universal acknowledgment among Bible interpreters,[41] its

36. Hurtado, *Lord Jesus Christ: Devotion to Jesus in Earliest Christianity* (Grand Rapids: Eerdmans, 2003), 50; see also Hurtado, *One God, One Lord.*

37. Bauckham, *Jesus and the God of Israel.*

38. Chris Tilling, *Paul's Divine Christology* (Grand Rapids: Eerdmans, 2015); Wright, *Paul and the Faithfulness of God*, 653–56.

39. R. Kendall Soulen, *The Divine Name(s) and the Holy Trinity*, vol. 1, *Distinguishing the Voices* (Louisville: Westminster John Knox, 2011), 211.

40. C. Kavin Rowe, "Biblical Pressure and Trinitarian Hermeneutics," *Pro Ecclesia* 11 (2002): 295–312; Rowe, "Romans 10:13: What Is the Name of the Lord?" *Horizons in Biblical Theology* 22 (2000): 135–73; Gordon D. Fee, *Pauline Christology: An Exegetical-Theological Study* (Grand Rapids: Baker Academic, 2013); Richard B. Hays, *Echoes of Scripture in the Gospels* (Waco: Baylor University Press, 2016).

41. See Carey C. Newman, James R. Davila, and Gladys S. Lewis, eds., *The Jewish Roots of Christological Monotheism: Papers from the St. Andrews Conference on the Historical Origins of the Worship of Jesus*, Supplements to the Journal for the Study of Judaism (Leiden: Brill, 1999); and, more recently, J. Daniel Kirk, *A Man Attested by God: The Human Jesus of the Synoptic Gospels* (Grand Rapids: Eerdmans, 2016).

presence is difficult to refute, especially in light of the preceding studies. For this reason, there is more reason now than there was two decades ago to affirm David Yeago's seminal thesis that while the New Testament does not use the *concepts* of the Nicene Creed to declare that Jesus is consubstantial with the Father it does render the same *judgment* through its monotheistic pattern of divine naming.[42]

A RELATIONAL PATTERN OF DIVINE NAMING

> For us there is one God, the Father, ... and one Lord, Jesus Christ. (1 Cor 8:6)

The second pattern of divine naming that 1 Corinthians 8:6 attests is a relational pattern of divine naming. In this pattern, the primary Trinitarian language of the Bible *distinguishes* God, Jesus, and the Spirit from one another *by means of their mutual relations*. First Corinthians 8:6 exemplifies this pattern in identifying God as "the Father" of Jesus Christ, who is by implication identified as God's "Son." The second pattern of divine naming does not benefit from the sheer quantity of studies that our first pattern enjoys. Nevertheless, a couple of important studies are worthy of mention.

Building on programmatic essays by Nils Dahl, Leander Keck, and Francis Watson,[43] and attentive to potential contributions from the history of biblical interpretation, two recent studies consider what the *relations* between God, Jesus, and the Spirit reveal about the identity of the Triune God.[44] In his book *The*

42. David S. Yeago, "The New Testament and the Nicene Dogma: A Contribution to the Recovery of Theological Exegesis," *Pro Ecclesia* 3 (1994): 152–64.

43. Nils Dahl, "The Neglected Factor in New Testament Theology," *Reflection* 73 (1975): 5–8; Leander Keck, "Toward the Renewal of New Testament Christology," *NTS* 32 (1986): 362–77; Francis Watson, "The Triune Divine Identity: Reflections on Pauline God-Language, in Disagreement with J. D. G. Dunn," *JSNT* 23 (2001): 99–124.

44. The following two paragraphs are adapted from my review of Bates's and Hill's books in *IJST* 19 (2017): 110–12.

Birth of the Trinity,[45] Matthew Bates addresses the emergence of Trinitarian doctrine in the early church, focusing on the role played by prosopological exegesis in the doctrine's development. In prosopological exegesis, a reading strategy attested as early as the second century BC and employed by first-century AD authors such as Philo and Paul, the "riddle" of unnamed speakers in ancient texts is resolved through the identification of speakers by a text's interpreter. Bates observes this interpretive practice in the New Testament authors' interpretation of the Old Testament, especially the Psalms, as well as in postapostolic interpretation of the Bible. According to Bates, this exegetical method of "solution by person" best explains the emergence of the Trinitarian concept of "person" in the early church and better accounts for the development of creedal teaching on the Trinity and Christology than other theories of doctrinal development. Bates seeks to confirm his thesis by tracing the ways early Christians interpret conversations between the persons of the Trinity in various Old Testament texts, following the arc of a theodramatic plot from the Son's eternal generation from the Father, through his incarnate mission and crucifixion, to his praise for divine deliverance and exaltation at the Father's right hand.

Whereas Bates focuses on the dialogical relations of the Trinity as exhibited across the biblical canon and suggests a hermeneutical origin for the term "person" in Trinitarian theology, Wesley Hill's *Paul and the Trinity*[46] focuses more specifically on debates surrounding Pauline God-talk and retrieves a concept of "relation" that is fruitful for interpreting the Bible's relational pattern of divine naming. Hill argues that the binary of high and low Christology, though commonplace in the contemporary

45. Matthew W. Bates, *The Birth of the Trinity: Jesus, God, and Spirit in New Testament and Early Christian Interpretations of the Old Testament* (Oxford: Oxford University Press, 2015).

46. Wesley Hill, *Paul and the Trinity: Persons, Relations, and the Pauline Letters* (Grand Rapids: Eerdmans, 2015).

literature, is inadequate for making sense of Paul's language about God, Christ, and the Holy Spirit. In place of this binary, Hill attempts to retrieve the traditional category of relation. In doing so, he avoids the vague and impressionistic appeals to "relationality" that plague a familiar stream of modern Trinitarian thought and, by means of critical interaction with recent scholarship on pro-Nicene theology and particularly its Thomist appropriation, refines a concept of relation that enables him to account for two registers of Pauline discourse about God (that is, "redoublement"): discourse that indicates what God, Christ, and the Spirit hold in common as the one God of Israel and discourse by which they are distinguished from one another by means of relation. Conscientious of the threat of anachronism in applying later theological concepts to the interpretation of the Bible, Hill tests his refined concept of relation in the exegesis of key passages in the Pauline letters (Phil 2:6–11; 1 Cor 8:6; 15:24–28; among others). He concludes from his exegetical analysis that such texts are more faithfully mapped by these dual registers of discourse than by the categories of high or low Christology. According to Hill's analysis, the relations between God, Christ, and the Spirit are *mutual, asymmetrically ordered relations* that "do not compromise the fundamental 'oneness' or 'unity' that obtains between them."[47]

The studies of Bates and Hill do not detract from the monotheistic pattern of divine naming. In fact, they explicitly presuppose and affirm it. But they also demonstrate that, taken by itself, the monotheistic pattern of divine naming cannot account fully for the self-presentation of the Triune God in holy Scripture. The God who names himself as YHWH our God also names himself as Father, Son, and Holy Spirit. And so we confess that within the one Lord God there are three person who are distinguished

---

47. Hill, *Paul and the Trinity*, 81.

from one another by their mutual, asymmetrically ordered, dialogical relations.

A METAPHYSICAL PATTERN OF DIVINE NAMING

> For us there is one God, the Father, from whom are all things and for whom we exist, and one Lord, Jesus Christ, through whom are all things and through whom we exist. (1 Cor 8:6)

The third pattern of divine naming that 1 Corinthians 8:6 attests is a metaphysical pattern of divine naming.[48] In this pattern, the primary Trinitarian language of the Bible indicates that God, Jesus, and the Spirit *transcend the categories of creaturely being and creaturely naming*. First Corinthians 8:6 exemplifies this pattern in identifying God and Christ by means of the language of what Gregory Sterling calls "prepositional metaphysics."[49] God the Father and the Lord Jesus Christ are not two of the "things" about which the Bible speaks. They are the source and goal of "all things" about which the Bible speaks. As such, they transcend creaturely classifications of being and creaturely modes of naming.

The metaphysical pattern of divine naming is the most understudied pattern of divine naming among recent works on the Bible and the Trinity. It is still common to read that the Bible is not concerned with "the inner nature of the one God" but rather

---

48. As Steve Duby argues, the tradition typically distinguishes theology from metaphysics, with the former focusing on God and his works and the latter focusing on the being of creatures. Nevertheless, the tradition, following the example of the New Testament itself, has also seen fit to critically appropriate metaphysical language and concepts in its discourse concerning God even though God, strictly speaking, is not the subject of metaphysical discourse. See Steven J. Duby, *God in Himself: Scripture, Metaphysics, and the Task of Christian Theology*, Studies in Christian Doctrine and Scripture (Downers Grove, IL: IVP Academic, 2019), chapter 4.

49. Gregory Sterling, "Prepositional Metaphysics in Jewish Wisdom Speculation and Early Christian Liturgical Texts," *The Studia Philonica Annual* 9 (1997): 219–38.

with his relationships with his creatures.[50] Theologians such as Robert Jenson, Matthew Levering, and Thomas Joseph White have countered such a perspective, arguing (in different ways) that metaphysical questions are unavoidable in interpreting biblical teaching about the Trinity.[51] To admit their point, however true, is not yet to address the issue of whether the primary Trinitarian language of the Bible *itself* exhibits metaphysical patterns of divine naming that might inform the grammar of constructive theological discourse. I believe that it *does* and that it *should*, and I would appeal to a handful of recent studies in support of this conviction.

Andrea Saner's book, *"Too Much to Grasp,"*[52] offers a sustained theological interpretation of Exodus 3:13–15, God's foundational act of self-naming to Moses at the burning bush. The author surveys the decidedly antimetaphysical conclusions of modern critical approaches to these verses and argues that their preoccupation with etymology and religious-historical reconstruction imposes severe methodological limitations when it comes to interpreting the theological subject matter of the text. Convinced "that Old Testament studies would do well to take greater care in addressing ontological implications of Old Testament texts,"[53] Saner develops a more sophisticated approach to interpreting the literal sense of God's self-revelation in Exodus 3 through interaction with the work of Brevard Childs, Hans Frei, and Augustine. With this approach in hand, she provides a close reading of Exodus 3:13–15 within the context of the book of Exodus and the Pentateuch's

---

50. Wright, *Paul and the Faithfulness of God*, 624, 626, 627. Similarly, Beverly Roberts Gaventa, "Pentecost and Trinity," *Interpretation* 66 (2012): 14.

51. Robert W. Jenson, *Systematic Theology*, 2 vols. (New York: Oxford University Press, 1997–99); Levering, *Scripture and Metaphysics*; Thomas Joseph White, *The Incarnate Lord: A Thomistic Study in Christology* (Washington, DC: Catholic University of America Press, 2015).

52. Andrea D. Saner, *"Too Much to Grasp": Exodus 3:13–15 and the Reality of God*, Journal of Theological Interpretation Supplements 11 (Winona Lake, IN: Eisenbrauns, 2015).

53. Saner, *"Too Much to Grasp,"* 230.

portrayal of Moses's role as covenant mediator. She concludes that God's self-naming in verse 14 functions as a "wordplay" and commentary on the Tetragrammaton. According to Saner, the self-referential nature of Exodus 3:14's wordplay—"I am who I am"—indicates the Tetragrammaton's transcendence of ordinary patterns of creaturely naming. The Tetragrammaton is neither a definition for God, identifying God's essence by means of genus and differentia, nor is it a proper name for God, picking God out as one individual within a larger class. Nevertheless, while Exodus 3:14 manifests God's transcendence of creaturely modes of naming, its purpose is not ultimately to hide YHWH from his people but to disclose his transcendent uniqueness as the self-subsisting one and to make YHWH "available to Israel" as the One on whose name they may call and as the One they may trust to fulfill his covenant promises in history.[54]

Approaches such as Saner's,[55] which are attentive to correspondences between the Bible's unique manner of naming God and God's unique manner of being and acting, help us better appreciate other examples of the metaphysical pattern of divine naming that are present in the Septuagint and the Greek New Testament. This is true whether those patterns are found in the Septuagint's translation of Exodus 3:14 and the New Testament's various appropriations of that translation[56] or the New Testament's various ways of actualizing central features of the broader Greco-Roman philosophical and theological cultural encyclopedia, such as the language of negative theology and causal metaphysics.[57]

---

54. Saner, *"Too Much to Grasp,"* 229.

55. See also Michael Allen, "Exodus 3," in *Theological Commentary: Evangelical Perspectives*, ed. R. Michael Allen (London: T&T Clark, 2011), chapter 3.

56. On which, see Sean M. McDonough, *YHWH at Patmos: Rev. 1:4 in Its Hellenistic and Early Jewish Setting*, WUNT 2/107 (Tübingen: Mohr Siebeck, 1999).

57. On New Testament appropriation of the language of negative theology, see Jerome Neyrey, "'Without Beginning of Days or End of Life' (Hebrews 7:3): Topos for a True Deity," *Catholic Biblical Quarterly* 53 (1991): 439–55. On New Testament appropriation of the language of causal metaphysics, see Robert Grant, "Causation and 'the

As noted above, 1 Corinthians 8:6 provides a specific example of this sort of actualization in using the language of prepositional metaphysics to describe God the Father and the Lord Jesus Christ as the sole first and final cause of "all things."[58]

The Bible's metaphysical pattern of divine naming identifies the Triune God as the self-subsistent source and goal of all things. In identifying the Trinity in this manner, the metaphysical pattern of divine naming indicates that both the oneness that binds the three persons together as well as the relations by which the three persons are distinguished exist and operate in a manner that transcends the categories of creaturely being, understanding, and language. Unfortunately, attention to the Bible's metaphysical pattern of divine naming is not a central feature of contemporary Trinitarian biblical exegesis, and this explains in part the often flat-and wrong-footed character of much contemporary Trinitarian theology. As the preceding discussion suggests, neglect of metaphysical analysis in biblical interpretation is not simply a failure to grapple with the subject matter of the biblical text. It is also a failure to attend to the forms of biblical discourse. For theology to speak *fluently* of the Trinity, it must speak *metaphysically*[59] of the Trinity, not just as a matter of drawing good and necessary consequences from the Bible, but as a matter of keeping in step with the Bible's primary Trinitarian language.[60]

Ancient World View,'" *JBL* 83 (1964): 34–40; and Sterling, "Prepositional Metaphysics." For further discussion of Jewish and early Christian use of Greco-Roman philosophical and theological terminology, see Scott R. Swain, *The God of the Gospel: Robert Jenson's Trinitarian Theology*, Strategic Initiatives in Evangelical Theology (Downers Grove, IL: IVP Academic, 2013), 173–79.

58. See Andrey Romanov, "Through One Lord Only: Theological Interpretation of the Meaning of διά in 1 Cor 8,6," *Biblica* 93 (2015): 391–415.

59. In the sense described in note 48 above—namely, critically appropriating metaphysical language and concepts to speak of the One who transcends the subject matter of metaphysics (that is, creaturely being).

60. In learning to follow the lead of the Bible's primary Trinitarian language, contemporary biblical exegetes and theologians may find assistance from patristic, medieval, and Reformation biblical exegetes and theologians, for whom the monotheistic, relational,

CALL ON HIS NAME

Christians confess the holy Trinity on the basis of holy Scripture. The Triune God adumbrates and attests himself to us in holy Scripture through foundational revelatory acts of divine self-naming that in turn endow a community of divine naming. Attending to the Bible's primary Trinitarian language reveals three patterns of divine naming that recur across various literary forms and across various redemptive-historical epochs. A monotheistic pattern of divine naming identifies the three persons with YHWH the one God of Israel; a relational pattern of divine naming distinguishes the three persons by means of their mutual, asymmetrically ordered, dialogical relations; and a metaphysical pattern of divine naming indicates that the three persons transcend the categories of creaturely being, understanding, and naming.

The one God who presents himself to us in holy Scripture as Father, Son, and Holy Spirit identifies himself as the self-subsistent source and goal of all things. In doing so, he calls us to epistemological and hermeneutical humility, reminding us that he is unlike any of the things that we meet, or of which we speak, in creation. "There is no one like the LORD our God" (Exod 8:10). In doing so, he also invites us to call on his name with confidence—in prayer, proclamation, and praise, as well as in the theological disciplines of biblical exegesis and dogmatics. The one God who names himself in holy Scripture as Father, Son, and Holy Spirit gives his name to us that, by the same Spirit, we may confess, "Jesus is Lord" (1 Cor 12:3), and cry, "Abba! Father!" (Gal 4:6). And so, by the Spirit, we confess with prophets and apostles and

---

and metaphysical patterns of divine naming were often a central feature of theological interpretation of holy Scripture. The work of retrieval is not easy. Nor is it without its dangers. And traditional patterns and practices of biblical exegesis sometimes run counter to the canons of modern biblical criticism. Nevertheless, the work of retrieval is worth it: learning to better follow biblical patterns of divine naming holds great promise for leading us more deeply into the knowledge and love of the Triune God who presents himself to us in holy Scripture.

with the church throughout the ages, "For us there is one God, the Father, from whom are all things and for whom we exist, and one Lord, Jesus Christ, through whom are all things and through whom we exist." To this great God, Father, Son, and Holy Spirit, be honor and glory forever and ever, world without end. Amen.

B. B. WARFIELD AND THE BIBLICAL DOCTRINE OF THE TRINITY

A HISTORICAL EXPERIMENT

What does it mean to say that the doctrine of the Trinity is a biblical doctrine?[1] Benjamin Breckinridge Warfield's "Trinity" entry in *The International Standard Bible Encyclopedia* (*ISBE*) provides an instructive response to this question.[2] Originally published in 1915, within a largely Ritschlian context that regarded doctrines like the Trinity as later corruptions of an originally undogmatic Christian religion,[3] Warfield's article presents his mature account of the biblical bases of the church's

---

1. Based on my inaugural lecture as professor of systematic theology at Reformed Theological Seminary, Orlando, Florida, delivered in the Pamplin Chapel on October 20, 2015. I am grateful to Michael Allen, Robert Cara, Graham Shearer, Fred Sanders, and Dolf te Velde for comments offered on an earlier draft of this article.

2. B. B. Warfield, "Trinity," in *The International Standard Bible Encyclopedia*, ed. James Orr (Chicago: Howard-Severance, 1915), 5:3012–22. Warfield's "Trinity" article was republished in numerous venues, including: Warfield, *Biblical Doctrines* (New York: Oxford, 1929), 133–72; Warfield, *Biblical and Theological Studies* (Philadelphia: Presbyterian & Reformed, 1952), 22–59; and Warfield, *Biblical Foundations* (Grand Rapids: Eerdmans, 1958), 79–116. Note that throughout the present essay, I have replaced Warfield's original abbreviations of terms with full terms and used contemporary conventions of capitalization.

3. Fred G. Zaspel, *The Theology of B. B. Warfield: A Systematic Summary* (Wheaton: Crossway, 2010), 185.

Trinitarian confession. Warfield examines the major biblical texts from which the doctrine of the Trinity is drawn. He surveys Old Testament passages commonly adduced by the "older writers" (for example, Gen 1:26; Num 6:24, 26; Ps 110:1; Prov 8), as well as those adduced by "more recent authors," including texts that portray the operation of a threefold divine cause in "the first ... and the second creation" (for example, Ps 33:6; Isa 61:1; 63:9–12; Hag 2:5–6).[4] Warfield also surveys various New Testament passages, considering the contributions of the Synoptic Gospels, the Johannine and Pauline writings, and the Catholic Epistles to Trinitarian doctrine. In each instance, he is careful to acknowledge the distinctive idiom of each New Testament author and to defend the authenticity of key Trinitarian prooftexts (for example, the Trinitarian baptismal formula of Matt 28:19).[5]

Warfield's *ISBE* entry on the Trinity is not merely an examination of Trinitarian prooftexts. Over the course of the article, the Princeton theologian offers a series of sophisticated judgments regarding the underlying hermeneutical logic that informs, and is informed by, exegesis of those texts. He discusses the legitimacy of using extrabiblical terminology to convey biblical teaching, the role of reason in Trinitarian doctrine, the relationship between the Old and New Testaments within the Trinitarian economy of revelation, and the variety and significance of biblical terminology in relation to its Triune referent. Ultimately, according to Warfield, the *doctrine* of the Triune God follows from the *revelation* of the Triune God in the *redemptive work* of the Triune God. In other words, the doctrine of the Trinity is revealed to us "in the incarnation of God the Son and the outpouring of God the Holy Spirit."[6] The New Testament is the literary sign that the early

4. Warfield, "Trinity," 3014.

5. Warfield, "Trinity," 3014–20.

6. Warfield, "Trinity," 3015. A few years before the publication of his *ISBE* article, Warfield made a similar methodological point: "The Trinity has been revealed to us only in the manifestations of the Son and Spirit in the persons of Jesus Christ and the Paraclete

church embraced this revelation of the Triune Redeemer and the literary expression of its universal Trinitarian consciousness.[7]

Warfield summarizes the main lines of biblical teaching on the Trinity in three points: (1) "there is but one God," (2) "the Father and the Son and the Spirit is each God," and (3) "the Father and the Son and the Spirit is each a distinct person." "When we have said these three things," he insists, "we have enunciated the doctrine of the Trinity in its completeness."[8] Warfield's summary is unremarkable when placed alongside later Reformed and evangelical syntheses of the doctrine. Wayne Grudem, for example, basically repeats Warfield's three-point summary in his *Systematic Theology*, as does Robert Reymond.[9] Viewed in relation to earlier statements of the doctrine, however, including those of Warfield's Presbyterian Church,[10] his summary lacks the completeness he claims for it. Specifically, Warfield omits any mention of the personal properties that distinguish the divine persons from one another—namely, the Father's eternal begetting of the Son ("paternity"), the Son's eternal generation from the Father ("filiation"), and the Spirit's eternal procession from the Father and the Son ("spiration").

Although his views are not without precedent in North American Presbyterianism and the broader Reformed tradition,

---

whom he has sent; and we obtain our only knowledge of the nature of the persons in the Trinity from the manifestations of personality in these persons. It is the Christological conception of personality, in other words, which must rule in constructing our Trinitarian conception of person; to this extent our theology must be Christo-centric" (Warfield, review of *Von der Gottheit Christi: Gegen den religiösen Rückschritt in Grüzmachers Dreieinigkeitslehre* by D. Karl Thieme, *Princeton Theological Review* 10 [1912]: 344).

7. Warfield, "Trinity," 3015.

8. Warfield, "Trinity," 3016.

9. Wayne Grudem, *Systematic Theology* (Grand Rapids: Zondervan, 1994), 226; Robert L. Reymond, *A New Systematic Theology of the Christian Faith*, 2nd ed. (Nashville: Thomas Nelson, 2010), chapter 8. A similar summary appears in Roger Nicole, "The Meaning of the Trinity," in *Standing Forth: Collected Writings of Roger Nicole* (Fearn, Ross-shire, UK: Christian Focus, 2002), 389.

10. Westminster Confession of Faith, chapter 2.3; Westminster Larger Catechism, question & answer 9–10.

this is a surprising omission to find in an article devoted to the biblical roots of Trinitarian doctrine. The personal properties reflect a broad ecclesiastical consensus in interpreting the revealed names into which we are baptized.[11] On the basis of the revealed names "Father," "Son," and "Holy Spirit," the church confesses that within the eternal depths of God's being there is one who stands in the relation of a father to a son, one who stands in the relation of a son to a father, and one who is breathed forth in the mutual love of the other two. Though surprising, this omission is not an oversight on Warfield's part. It is the result of reasoned, interpretive judgment. According to Warfield, the Son's eternal generation and the Spirit's eternal procession "are not implicates of their designation as Son and Spirit."[12]

The purpose in what follows is to consider Warfield's proposed revision to the traditional doctrine of the Trinity. The discussion will proceed in four steps. First, I will summarize Warfield's biblical argument against the personal properties. Second, I will locate Warfield's argument within the historical-theological trajectory of which it is a part. Third, I will respond to Warfield's argument by pointing to patterns of biblical teaching that challenge his interpretation and by addressing what seems to be Warfield's primary worries regarding eternal generation and eternal procession. Fourth and finally, my discussion will conclude with some observations on the importance of the traditional interpretation of the revealed names for Trinitarian theology.

---

11. Basil of Caesarea: "I think there is no doctrine in the gospel of our salvation more important than faith in the Father and the Son. ... We have been sealed in the Father and the Son through the grace received in baptism. Hence when he [Eunomius] dares to deny these terms, he simultaneously takes exception to the whole power of the gospels, proclaiming a Father who has not begotten and a Son who was not begotten" (*Against Eunomius*, trans. Mark DelCogliano and Andrew Radde-Gallwitz, Fathers of the Church 122 [Washington, DC: Catholic University of America Press, 2011], 2.22). On the place of the doctrine of eternal generation in pro-Nicene theology, see Lewis Ayres, *Nicaea and Its Legacy: An Approach to Fourth-Century Trinitarian Theology* (Oxford: Oxford University Press, 2004), 236.

12. Warfield, "Trinity," 3020.

WARFIELD'S REVISION IN ITS IMMEDIATE HISTORICAL CONTEXT

Warfield's proposed revision of Trinitarian doctrine may be better appreciated by comparing his summary of the doctrine with that of Charles Hodge, Warfield's predecessor as the chair of theology at Princeton. Hodge summarizes the "biblical form of the doctrine" in five points.[13]

Hodge's first three points are nearly identical to the three points we find in Warfield. His fourth and fifth points, however, include affirmations absent from Warfield's summary. (1) "There is one only living and true God." (2) "In the Bible, all divine titles and attributes are ascribed equally to the Father, Son, and Spirit." (3) "The Father, Son, and Spirit are distinct persons."[14] (4) Hodge affirms ordered modes of being and operation within the Trinity: "In the Holy Trinity there is a subordination of the Persons as to the mode of subsistence and operation."[15] (5) Hodge then specifies the nature of these ordered modes of being and operation. According to Hodge, the distinct modes of subsistence in the Trinity are reflected in the predication of "certain acts, or conditions" to "one person of the Trinity, which are never predicated of either of the others," such as "generation ... to the Father, filiation

---

13. Charles Hodge, *Systematic Theology*, 3 vols., repr. (Grand Rapids: Eerdmans, 1997), 1:443–45.

14. Hodge, *Systematic Theology*, 1:444.

15. As the context demonstrates, Hodge uses the term "subordination" in the Latinate sense of "ordered under," referring to the relations of origin that distinguish the persons from each other—that is, the fact that the Father personally exists and acts from himself, that the Son personally exists and acts from the Father, and that the Spirit personally exists and acts from the Father and the Son. (Note that "Subordination," for Hodge, does not describe an ordered relation of authority and submission among the persons of the Trinity, as some later theologians will come to use the term, but rather an order of subsistence within God's consubstantial being *ad intra* and indivisible operation *ad extra*.) Warfield, for reasons that will become clearer in section 3, seems to operate with a different sense of the term "subordination," assuming that it (and the relations of origin that the term traditionally signifies) connotes derivative, lesser status within the Godhead. As we will see below, Scripture and tradition give us ample reason to discount this assumption. See also footnote 52 below.

to the Son, and procession to the Spirit," while the distinct modes of operation are reflected in the way certain external operations, common to and indivisible among the persons of the Trinity, are nevertheless predominantly predicated of one person in particular. Thus, for example, "the Father creates, elects, and calls; the Son redeems; and the Spirit sanctifies."[16]

Though not included in his summary of biblical teaching on the Trinity, Warfield does affirm with Hodge the existence of ordered relations among the persons in their external modes of operation:

> There is, of course, no question that in "modes of operation," as it is technically called—that is to say, in the functions ascribed to the several persons of the Trinity in the redemptive process, and, more broadly, in the entire dealing of God with the world—the principle of subordination is clearly expressed. The Father is first, the Son is second, and the Spirit is third, in the operations of God as revealed to us in general, and very especially in those operations by which redemption is accomplished. Whatever the Father does, he does through the Son (Rom. ii. 16; iii. 22; v. 1, 11, 17, 21; Eph i. 5; I Thess. v. 9; Tit. iii. v) by the Spirit. The Son is sent by the Father and does his Father's will (Jn. vi. 38); the Spirit is sent by the Son and does not speak from himself, but only takes of Christ's and shows it unto his people (Jn. xvii. 7 ff.); and we have our Lord's own word for it that "one that is sent is not greater than he that sent him" (Jn. xiii. 16). In crisp decisiveness, our Lord even declares, indeed: "My Father is greater than I" (Jn. xiv. 28); and Paul tells us that Christ is God's, even as we are Christ's (I Cor. iii. 23), and that as Christ is "the head of every man," so God is "the head of Christ" (I Cor. xi. 3).[17]

---

16. Hodge, *Systematic Theology*, 1:445.
17. Warfield, "Trinity," 3020–21.

Warfield argues, nevertheless, that the order of operation among the persons "in the redemptive process" does not reflect a deeper reality within God's Triune life. In other words, Warfield denies that the Trinity's external modes of operation follow the Trinity's eternal modes of subsistence: that the Father's sending of the Son in time follows from the Father's begetting of the Son in eternity, that the Father and the Son's sending of the Spirit in time follows from the Father and the Son's breathing of the Spirit in eternity. He suggests instead that these ordered external operations follow only from "a convention, an agreement, between the persons of the Trinity—a 'covenant' as it is technically called—by virtue of which a distinct function in the work of redemption is voluntarily assumed by each," from "the humiliation of the Son of God for his work's sake," and from "the two natures in the constitution of his person as incarnated."[18] God's Triune *will*—as expressed in the covenant of redemption and in the Son's incarnate mission—rather than God's Triune *nature* determines his Triune mode of operation within the external economy of nature, grace, and glory.

From one vantage point, Warfield's sensibilities here are entirely sound. Christian theology must affirm that God's Triune will determines much about the character of the Triune economy. The alternative would be the perilous assumption that God necessarily creates, necessarily becomes incarnate, and necessarily indwells the church. Nevertheless, while Christian theology must affirm the *freedom* of creation, incarnation, and indwelling, it has typically affirmed also that God's external actions in creation, incarnation, and indwelling *correspond* in some way to realities that obtain within God's Triune life, that God's ordered modes of operation outside himself (*ad extra*) follow God's ordered modes of subsistence inside himself (*ad intra*). And it has affirmed that these ordered modes of subsistence are identifiable

18. Warfield, "Trinity," 3021.

by the personal properties of paternity, filiation, and spiration. This Warfield fails to affirm, and that for what he deems biblical reasons.

Contrary to broad Protestant and Catholic exegetical consensus, Warfield argues that the revealed names Father, Son, and Spirit do not signify the personal properties of paternity, filiation, and spiration. His argument is twofold. First, Warfield attempts to relativize the significance of these revealed names by pointing to broader patterns of Trinitarian naming in the New Testament. It may seem "natural ... to assume that the mutual relations of the persons of the Trinity are revealed in the designations, 'the Father, the Son, and the Holy Spirit,'" Warfield concedes, but the vast diversity of names used by New Testament writers to describe the divine persons and the varied orders in which the divine persons are described militate against this assumption.[19] In the Synoptic Gospels, and especially in the Johannine writings, the names Father, Son, and Spirit are common designations of the divine persons. In Paul and other New Testament authors, however, the names God, the Lord Jesus Christ, and the Holy Spirit are also common.[20] Moreover, he continues, the latter designations do not always follow the same order as that found, for example, in Matthew's baptismal formula, where the Father is named first, the Son is named second, and the Holy Spirit is named third (Matt 28:19). In the case of these other designations, sometimes the Lord Jesus Christ is named first (1 Cor 13:14) and sometimes the Spirit is named first (1 Cor 12:4–6; Eph 4:4–6).[21] Given the diverse pattern of Trinitarian naming in the New Testament, Warfield contends, we should not conclude that the names Father, Son, and Spirit exclusively indicate the nature of the divine persons' internal relations.

19. Warfield, "Trinity," 3020.

20. Warfield, "Trinity," 3019.

21. Warfield, "Trinity," 3020.

Second, Warfield argues that the traditional interpretation of the names Father, Son, and Holy Spirit has misunderstood their theological significance. Though his argument at this point is formally quite similar to that of Herman Alexander Röell, Thomas Ridgely, and several leading New England Congregationalist theologians, Warfield does not follow Röell, Ridgely, and others in arguing that these names merely describe the divine persons in terms of their economic relationships with creatures.[22] According to Warfield, the personal names signify "eternal and necessary relations."[23] What is the nature of these "eternal and necessary relations"? Warfield grants that it may be natural to assume the names Son and Spirit imply *relations of origin* among the divine persons—that is, relations in which the Father is the source of the Son through begetting and in which the Father and the Son are the source of the Spirit through breathing. "But," he insists, "it is quite certain that this was not the denotation of either term."[24] When one considers John 5:18 and 1 Corinthians 2:10–11—texts that provide nearly "formal definitions" of the terms "Son" and "Spirit" according to Warfield—the emphasis in both cases "is laid on the notion of equality or sameness."[25] Furthermore, Warfield attempts to demonstrate that other terms, such as "only begotten" (John 1:18) and "firstborn" (Col 1:15), "contain no implication of

22. We will return to Röell's views below. For Ridgely's arguments in this regard, see *A Body of Divinity: Wherein the Doctrines of the Christian Religion Are Explained and Defended, Being the Substance of Several Lectures on the Assembly's Larger Catechism*, 4 vols. (Philadelphia: W. W. Woodward, 1814), 1:259–60, 263, 266–70, 274, 277. For Moses Stuart, see *Letters on the Eternal Generation of the Son of God, Addressed to the Rev. Samuel Miller* (Andover: Mark Newman, 1822). Warfield interacts with these views in his "Calvin's Doctrine of the Trinity," in *Calvin and Calvinism (New York, NY: Oxford University Press, 1932; repr.*, Grand Rapids: Baker, 1981), chapter 4. According to James H. Moorhead, "[Moses] Stuart claimed he had never once heard [the doctrine of eternal generation] 'seriously avowed and defended' in New England" (Moorhead, *Princeton Seminary in American Religion and Culture* [Grand Rapids: Eerdmans, 2012], 70).

23. Warfield, "Trinity," 3021.

24. Warfield, "Trinity," 3020.

25. Warfield, "Trinity," 3020.

derivation" but instead indicate "unique consubstantiality" and "priority of existence."[26] Warfield's interpretive conclusion: "What underlies the conception of sonship in Scriptural speech is just 'likeness'; whatever the father is that the son is also." The same goes for the Holy Spirit.[27]

With these two arguments Warfield attempts to demonstrate that the ordered relations that characterize God's tripersonal action outside himself do not characterize God's tripersonal relations inside himself. Before addressing these two arguments, we should note what seems to be Warfield's major worry about affirming ordered relations of paternity, filiation, and spiration within God's Triune being. In his judgment, the personal properties of paternity, filiation, and spiration imply the existence of "derivation" and "subordination" within the Triune God and thereby compromise "the complete and undiminished deity of each of these persons."[28] For Warfield, the full equality and consubstantiality of the divine persons is ultimately at stake in interpreting the revealed names Father, Son, and Spirit.

Relative to Hodge's summary of Trinitarian doctrine, we may describe Warfield's as one characterized by a "principled non-affirmation" of the doctrines of the eternal generation of the Son and the eternal procession of the Spirit. Though Warfield does not explicitly *deny* these doctrines in his *ISBE* article,[29] he argues from multiple angles that biblical exegesis does not require us to *affirm* them. The discontinuity between Hodge and Warfield, however, should not be overstated. In his treatment of the doctrine of eternal generation, Hodge expresses a number of worries

---

26. Warfield, "Trinity," 3020.

27. Warfield, "Trinity," 3020.

28. Warfield, "Trinity," 3020, 3022. This motivation is also observed by Brannon Ellis, *Calvin, Classical Trinitarianism, and the Aseity of the Son* (Oxford: Oxford University Press, 2012), 8.

29. A point rightly emphasized by Fred G. Zaspel, "Benjamin Breckinridge Warfield on the Doctrine of the Trinity," *Southern Baptist Journal of Theology* 21, no. 2 (2017): 104–7.

about attempts by pro-Nicene theologians to explain the doctrine and ends up with an apophatic account that effectively drains the doctrine of much of its meaning.[30] Hodge's treatment of the doctrine of eternal generation, moreover, resonates with that of his Princeton colleague Samuel Miller who, in his defense of the doctrine against Moses Stuart's objections, expresses similar reservations regarding earlier explanations of the doctrine, including most notably that of Francis Turretin.[31] Warfield's "principled non-affirmation" of the doctrine of eternal generation thus represents a not unnatural development within a Princeton theological tradition already characterized by what we might call a "tepid affirmation" of the doctrine.

WARFIELD'S REVISION IN ITS BROADER HISTORICAL CONTEXT

Toward the conclusion of his *ISBE* article, Warfield offers a brief sketch of the history of Trinitarian doctrine. On his reading, the history of the doctrine exhibits a struggle between those who properly assert "the principle of equalization" among the persons of the Trinity and those who "unduly ... emphasize the elements of subordinationism which still hold a place ... in the traditional language in which the church states its doctrine."[32] Warfield identifies John Calvin among those who stand on the right side of this historical contest: "Calvin takes his place, alongside of Tertullian, Athanasius and Augustine, as one of the chief contributors to the exact and vital statement of the Christian doctrine of the triune God."[33] According to Warfield, Calvin's particular contribution to the Christian doctrine of the Trinity is "to reassert and make

30. Hodge, *Systematic Theology*, 1:468–73.

31. Samuel Miller, *Letters on the Eternal Sonship of Christ: Addressed to the Rev. Professor Stuart of Andover* (Philadelphia: W. W. Woodward, 1823), 34–36.

32. Warfield, "Trinity," 3022.

33. Warfield, "Trinity," 3022.

good the attribute of the self-existence of the Son."[34] Although Warfield's *ISBE* article does not fully indicate *how* Calvin's theology accomplishes this, his other writings do. Calvin's radical commitment to the aseity of the Son leads to a revision of the doctrine of eternal generation in the Reformer's own thought and lays the exegetical foundation that would eventually lead to wholesale rejection of the doctrine of eternal generation by later followers.[35] I believe Warfield's rejection of the personal properties of paternity, filiation, and spiration is best understood as an attempt to perfect this trajectory in Calvinian Trinitarianism.

As Richard Muller observes, the affirmation and defense of the Son's aseity is "the distinctive feature of Reformed trinitarianism."[36] According to common Reformed teaching, the Son not only possesses the divine attributes of eternity, immutability, omnipotence, and omnipresence, he also possesses the divine attribute of aseity. The Son is *autotheos*, God in and of himself. For Reformed theology, the affirmation of the Son's aseity is integral to the affirmation of the Son's consubstantiality with the Father. Because he is "equal with God" (John 5:19), the Son must have "life in himself" just "as the Father has life in himself" (v. 26).

The majority of theologians in the Reformed tradition argue that the aseity of the Son is consistent with the eternal generation of the Son from the Father. The consistency between these two aspects of the Son's person lies in properly distinguishing the Son's *being* (that which the Son holds in *common* with the Father and the Spirit) from his *mode of being* (that which *distinguishes* the Son from the Father and the Spirit). Because he is equal with

---

34. Warfield, "Trinity," 3022.

35. Warfield, "Calvin's Doctrine of the Trinity," 276–77.

36. Richard Muller, *Post-Reformation Reformed Dogmatics: The Rise and Development of Reformed Orthodoxy, ca. 1520 to ca. 1725*, Vol. 4, *The Triunity of God* (Grand Rapids: Baker Academic, 2003), 324. For development and debate, see Ellis, *Calvin*. For debate at the Westminster Assembly, see Chad Van Dixhoorn, "Post-Reformation Trinitarian Perspectives," in *Retrieving Eternal Generation*, ed. Fred Sanders and Scott R. Swain (Grand Rapids: Zondervan Academic, 2017), chapter 10.

God *in being* (John 5:19), the Son has "life in himself" just "as the Father has life in himself" (v. 6). Because he is distinct from the Father *in his mode of being*, the Son has "life in himself" as something eternally "granted" or communicated to him by the Father (v. 26). For these theologians, it is precisely the Son's *distinct mode of being* as one eternally begotten of the Father that accounts for his *being consubstantial* with the Father.[37] Thus Francis Turretin:

> As all generation indicates a communication of essence on the part of the begetter to begotten (by which the begotten becomes like the begetter and partakes of the same nature with him), so this wonderful generation is rightly expressed as a communication of essence from the Father (by which the Son possesses indivisibly the same essence with him and is made perfectly like him).[38]

Though he does not reject the doctrine of eternal generation per se, Calvin's commitment to the Son's aseity does lead him to revise the doctrine considerably. For Calvin and the significant minority of Reformed theologians who follow him on this issue, the eternal generation of the Son from the Father involves no "communication of essence" to the Son by the Father.[39] Accordingly, texts like John 5:26, which speaks of the Father "granting" aseity to the

---

37. Representative statements include Zacharias Ursinus, *Commentary on the Heidelberg Catechism*, trans. G. W. Willard, repr. ed. (Phillipsburg, NJ: Presbyterian & Reformed, 1985), 130–32, 135–36, 181–84; Jerome Zanchi, *De Tribus Elohim* (Frankfurt am Main, 1572), I, 5.7.4 (p. 222, col. 2); Dolf te Velde, ed., *Synopsis of a Purer Theology*, vol. 1 (Leiden: Brill, 2014), 8.7, 18; James Ussher, *A Body of Divinity: Or, the Sum and Substance of the Christian Religion*, ed. Michael Nevarr, repr. ed. (Birmingham: Solid Ground Christian Books, 2007), 69–70; John Owen, ΧΡΙΣΤΟΛΟΓΙΑ: Or, A Declaration of the Glorious Mystery of the Person of Christ—God and Man, in *The Works of John Owen*, ed. William H. Goold (Edinburgh: Banner of Truth, 1965), 1:71–72.

38. Francis Turretin, *Institutes of Elenctic Theology*, trans. George Musgrave Giger (Phillipsburg, NJ: Presbyterian & Reformed, 1992), 1:293.

39. John Calvin, *Institutes of the Christian Religion*, trans. Ford Lewis Battles (Philadelphia: Westminster, 1960), 1.13.19–29; with Scott R. Swain, "The Trinity in the Reformers," in *The Oxford Handbook of the Trinity*, ed. Gilles Emery and Matthew Levering (Oxford: Oxford University Press, 2011), 235; and more fully Ellis, *Calvin*.

Son, are not interpreted with reference to the eternal relationship between the Father and the Son but with reference to the temporal, economic relationship between the Father and the Son in his office as incarnate mediator. The Genevan Reformer considers a properly Trinitarian exegesis of this verse "harsh and far-fetched." In his judgment, the focus of John 5:26 is the Son of God only "so far as he is manifested in the flesh."[40]

Calvin's precedent in revising the doctrine of eternal generation and his pattern of exegetical reasoning provide the foundation for "the more advanced position" on eternal generation that Warfield finds in Herman Alexander Röell (1653–1718).[41] Röell, professor at Franeker and then Utrecht in the late seventeenth and early eighteenth centuries, was a leading synthesizer of Cartesian rationalism and Reformed theology.[42] Building on a notion of divine perfection derived from his Cartesian natural thelogy and eager to avoid the subordinationist tendencies he detected in Arminian and Socinian thought,[43] Röell elevated the Calvinian commitment to divine aseity to the level of critical principle for Trinitarian theology. The effect was to exclude any conception of communication or origination, whether in being or mode of being, from God's Triune life.[44] Where the majority of Reformed theologians had confessed a self-existent Son *because*

---

40. John Calvin, *Commentary on the Gospel according to John*, trans. William Pringle (Grand Rapids : Eerdmans, 1956; repr.,), 1:198–207. On Calvin's general reticence toward Trinitarian reflection in his exegesis of classical Trinitarian prooftexts, see Arie Baars, *Om Gods verhevenheid en Zijn nabijheid: De Drie-eenheid bij Calvijn* (Kampen: Kok, 2004), 291–308.

41. Warfield, "Calvin's Doctrine of the Trinity," 276–77. Compare Warfield's judgment with Miller's estimation of Röell vis-à-vis Turretin's views of eternal generation in *Letters on the Eternal Sonship of Christ*, 34–36.

42. For fuller discussion of Röell's views, see Ellis, *Calvin*, 224–40.

43. For the influence of Arminian and Socinian views of the Trinity on Reformed formulations of the doctrine, see Muller, *Triunity of God*, 328–32.

44. Herman Alexander Röell, *De Generatione Filii et Morte Fidelium Temporali* (Franeker: Gyselaar, 1689); and Röell, *Explicatio Catecheseos Heidelbergensis: Opus Posthumum* (Utrecht, 1728), 175–84, 259–71; with Warfield, "Calvin's Doctrine of the Trinity," 276; and Ellis, *Calvin*, 237–38.

they confessed an only-begotten Son and where Calvin had confessed a self-existent Son *alongside* the (modified) confession of an only-begotten Son, Röell forced theology to choose *between* a self-existent Son and an only-begotten Son.

As noted earlier, Warfield does not follow Röell and others in limiting the meaning of the personal names of the Trinity to their significance within the economy of salvation. It seems, however, that Warfield ultimately accepts Röell's dilemma regarding aseity and eternal generation and that he is willing to sacrifice the confession of "begotten not made" on the altar of "consubstantial with the Father."

Before moving on, it is worth pausing to observe a few points. First, the relationship between divine aseity and divine persons is far from self-evident—even among those who share similar Reformed theological sensibilities! Second, the implications of divine aseity for the nature of divine persons is internally related to the question of whether the derivation (certainly an unhappy term) of one divine person from another divine person entails equality or inferiority. As we have seen, for the majority of Reformed theologians derivation is the root of equality and thus a ground for confessing the full deity of Christ; for the Calvinian minority of Reformed theologians, which includes Warfield, derivation is evidence of inferiority and thus a threat to an orthodox christological confession. Third and finally, theological judgments regarding each of the aforementioned issues rest on exegetical judgments about the interpretation of various Trinitarian prooftexts and hermeneutical judgments about which prooftexts count as relevant to the discussion.

RESPONSE TO WARFIELD'S REVISION

According to Warfield, the revealed names Father, Son, and Spirit do not signify the personal properties of paternity, filiation, and spiration. What should we make of this interpretive claim?

Warfield's first argument against the traditional interpretation is that the New Testament uses a wide variety of names in varied orders to describe the Trinity. This argument, however, is not problematic for the traditional interpretation of the personal names Father, Son, and Spirit. The variety of names and varied orders of naming that appear in the New Testament neither relativize nor undermine the traditional interpretation. As we will see below, the New Testament often employs additional names for the Trinity in order to further specify the meaning of the names Father, Son, and Spirit. Moreover, though Paul commonly identifies the Triune persons from the perspective of the relations in which they stand to creatures (for example, "God," "Lord Jesus Christ") rather than from the relations in which they stand to each other (for example, "Father," "Son"), this pattern is not absolute. The apostle also uses descriptions that combine the persons' relations to creatures with their relations to each other, and, when he does, these combinations reinforce the significance of the personal names Father, Son, and Spirit. Thus, for example, Paul regularly identifies the first person of the Trinity as "the God and Father of our Lord Jesus Christ" (Rom 15:6; 2 Cor 1:3; Eph 1:3; Col 1:3; see also 1 Pet 1:3). And he identifies the Spirit as "the Spirit of [God's] Son" (Gal 4:6) and as "the Spirit of sonship" (Rom 8:15), who enables us to call God, "Abba! Father!" (Gal 4:6). Finally, the fact that the persons appear in varied syntactical orders in the New Testament writings hardly supports Warfield's criticism of the traditional interpretation of the personal names of the Trinity. Syntactical order should not be confused with personal order. Though Jesus Christ appears syntactically before God and the Holy Spirit in 2 Corinthians 13:14, the appropriation of "grace" to Jesus Christ, "love" to God, and "fellowship" to the Holy Spirit indicates that, in Paul's mind, God's Triune saving agency proceeds from God's loving impulse, through the gracious gift of Jesus Christ and culminating in the fellowship of the Holy Spirit. This ordered mode of operation in God's Triune saving agency does not contradict but confirms a traditional understanding of the ordered modes of being among the persons of the Trinity.

Warfield's second argument against the traditional interpretation of the personal names is that in Scripture the names Son and Spirit connote likeness, equality, and sameness with the Father rather than derivation from the Father. This argument also runs into problems upon closer analysis. In biblical idiom—whether it be Trinitarian or non-Trinitarian contexts, literal or metaphorical contexts—relations of origin are not opposed to likeness; relations of origin regularly constitute the basis for likeness. In Genesis 5:3, Adam "fathers" Seth "in his own likeness, after his image." In this paradigmatic instance of literal fathering, natural *likeness* between Adam the father and Seth the son is traceable to the relation of origin whereby Adam *begets* Seth. Likewise, even in metaphorical cases of fathering, where there is metaphysical disproportion between father and offspring, the link between begetting and likeness is preserved and emphasized. In the Davidic covenant, the right of the Davidic heir to rule on earth as YHWH rules in heaven follows from the fact that YHWH has "begotten" him as his son, thus constituting him the heir of God's family business (2 Sam 7:12–14; Ps 2:6–9). In similar fashion, though there is infinite metaphysical disproportion between God and the created lights that he has produced and placed in the heavens, James 1:17 perceives in the created lights a filial resemblance to the "Father of lights, with whom there is no variation or shadow due to change." Again, in metaphorical contexts of begetting as in literal contexts, resemblance is rooted in relations of origin.[45]

---

45. For further discussion of this point, see Scott R. Swain, "The Radiance of the Father's Glory: Eternal Generation, the Divine Names, and Biblical Interpretation," in *Retrieving Eternal Generation*, ed. Fred Sanders and Scott R. Swain (Grand Rapids: Zondervan Academic, 2017), 36–40.

What is true in non-Trinitarian contexts of begetting, both literal and metaphorical, is true in Trinitarian contexts as well. Leaving aside the question of how we should translate μονογενής (various options include "one of a kind," "only begotten," and "only child"), consider three examples of how the New Testament portrays the Father-Son relation as a relation as a *relation of origin*, with the Father being the principle or source of the Son's person or agency, and *ontological equality*, with the Son sharing the selfsame nature and agency of the Father.[46]

LLUSTRATIONS OF THE FATHER-SON RELATION

The New Testament employs a number of illustrations, what Athanasius calls *paradeigmata*,[47] that further amplify the nature of the relation that obtains between the Father and the Son. These additional names for the Son are not merely ornamental. They function as indispensable conceptual tools that help faith contemplate more fully the (ultimately incomprehensible) nature of the Father-Son relation.[48] Drawing on Old Testament and other Jewish wisdom literature (for example, Prov 8; Wis 7:26), the New Testament portrays the Son as the "radiance" of the Father's glory (Heb 1:3), as the "image" of the invisible God (Col 1:15), and as the "Word" of God (John 1:1; Rev 19:13). In each instance, these illustrations indicate complete ontological correspondence between the Father and the Son: the Word of God is God

46. In the following two paragraphs, I draw from Scott R. Swain, "Divine Trinity," in *Christian Dogmatics: Reformed Theology for the Church Catholic*, ed. Michael Allen and Scott R. Swain (Grand Rapids: Baker Academic, 2016), 88–90.

47. On which, see Khaled Anatolios, *Athanasius*, Early Church Fathers (London: Routledge, 2004), 62–67; and Anatolios, *Retrieving Nicaea: The Development and Meaning of Trinitarian Doctrine* (Grand Rapids: Baker Academic, 2011), 110–14.

48. Athanasius, *Letters to Serapion on the Holy Spirit*, in *Works on the Spirit: Athanasius and Didymus*, trans. Mark DelCogliano, Andrew Radde-Gallwitz, and Lewis Ayres, Popular Patristics (Crestwood, NY: St. Vladimir's Seminary Press, 2011), 1.19–20.

(John 1:1); the image of the invisible God stands on the Creator side of the Creator-creature divide as the One by whom, in whom, and for whom creation exists (Col 1:16–17); the radiance of God is the exact imprint of the Father's substance (Heb 1:3). These illustrations also indicate that ontological correspondence between the Father and the Son obtains within the context of a relation of origin wherein the Father is the principle or source of the Son, who is his perfect Word, image, and radiance.

GOD'S UNIQUE NAME/NATURE AND THE FATHER-SON RELATION

The New Testament also indicates that the Father and the Son share the unique divine name and nature within the context of a relation characterized by giving on the part of the Father and receiving on the part of the Son. According to John 17:11 and Philippians 2:9–11, the Father has given his "name" to the Son. According to John 5:26, the Father has granted the Son to have "life in himself" just as the Father has "life in himself."

GOD'S EXTERNAL ACTIONS AND THE FATHER-SON RELATION

Finally, the New Testament in various ways displays God's external actions toward his creatures as expressing the ordered relation of the Father and the Son. In God's creative and providential activity, the Father acts *through* the Son (John 1:3; 1 Cor 8:6; Col 1:16), and the Son acts *from* the Father (John 5:19). In similar fashion, the Son's mission to become incarnate and make atonement is a mission he fulfills in obedience to the Father who sent him (Mark 12:1–12; John 6:38; Gal 4:4–5), and the Son's enthronement as king is an authority he receives from his Father (Matt 11:27; 28:18; Eph 1:20–23; Heb 1:3–4; with Ps 110). In each of these instances, we are not dealing with a distinction between God's action and the action of a creature. We are dealing with God's unique divine action as Creator, providential Ruler, Redeemer, and Lord, and with a distinction that obtains *within* this unique divine action: a distinction that expresses the ordered relation of the Father and the Son. Similar patterns of divine naming characterize the Spirit's relation to the Father and the Son as well.

ILLUSTRATIONS OF THE SPIRIT'S RELATION TO THE FATHER AND THE SON

The New Testament employs several paradigms or illustrations that amplify the unique nature of the Spirit's relationship to the Father and the Son. As in the case of the Father-Son relation, a number of these illustrations are drawn from the Old Testament (for example, Isa 44:3; Joel 2:28; Ezek 47:1–12). Particularly instructive are illustrations that associate the Holy Spirit with water. The Spirit is identified as one who is "poured out" by the Father (Rom 5:5) and by the Son (Acts 2:33), as the element with which Jesus baptizes his disciples (Mark 1:8; 1 Cor 12:13), and as the living water that flows "from the throne of God and of the Lamb" (Rev 22:1). This rich web of imagery at once identifies the Spirit as the divine source of life and as the one who, in his life-giving identity and mission, proceeds from the Father and the Son.

GOD'S UNIQUE NAME/NATURE AND THE SPIRIT'S RELATION TO THE FATHER AND THE SON

The New Testament also indicates the nature of the Spirit's relation to the Father and the Son by virtue of the Spirit's relation to God's unique name and nature. As the Father gives the divine name to the Son, so the Spirit (who also shares the divine name: 2 Cor 3:17) causes the Son to be acknowledged as "Lord" (1 Cor 12:3), to the glory of God the Father (Phil 2:11). Similarly, while the Spirit *is* "the truth" (1 John 5:6), he is also the Spirit "*of* truth" (1 John 4:6).

Consequently, he is able to guide Jesus' disciples "into all the truth" (John 16:13) because of the unique relation in which he stands to the Father and the Son: he does not speak "from himself" but only what "he hears" (v. 13), taking what he holds in common with the Son and with the Father and declaring it to the apostles (vv. 14–15).[49] When it comes to divine truth, therefore, the distinction between the Spirit and the Father and the Son "is not in what is had, but in the order of having."[50]

GOD'S EXTERNAL ACTIONS AND THE SPIRIT'S RELATION TO THE FATHER AND THE SON

Finally, as in the case of the Father and the Son, the Spirit's ordered relation to the Father and the Son is expressed in God's external actions toward his creatures. The Father and the Son work *through* the Spirit: the Father gives the Holy Spirit to those who ask him (Luke 11:13), and Jesus performs miracles "by the Spirit of God" (Matt 12:28). Moreover, as the Father sends the Son to accomplish his incarnate mission, in similar fashion the Father and the Son send the Spirit to indwell God's children (John 14:26; 15:26; 16:7; Gal 4:6) in order that, through the Son, Jew and Gentile might have access "in one Spirit to the Father" (Eph 2:18; with 1:23 and 5:18). Once again, an observable pattern emerges: The distinction between the activity of the Spirit toward creatures and the activity of the Father and the Son toward creatures is not a distinction between creaturely action and a divine action. The distinction between the three is a distinction that is internal to the singular divine action whereby Triune God fulfills his ancient covenant promise to dwell among his people forever (John 14:16–17, 23; with Lev 26:12), and that manifests the Spirit's

49. Didymus the Blind, *On the Holy Spirit*, in DelCogliano, Radde-Gallwitz, and Ayres, *Works on the Spirit*, 170–74.

50. Thomas Aquinas, *Commentary on the Gospel of John, Chapters 13–21*, trans. Fabian Larcher and James Weisheipl (Washington, DC: Catholic University of America Press, 2010), 145.

ordered relation to the Father and the Son. In the coming of the Triune God to dwell among us, the Spirit comes from the Father through the Son and leads us through the Son to the Father.

One might object that many of the aforementioned examples of Trinitarian naming refer to the persons within the economy of salvation, not to their eternal relations. However, while many of these examples speak of the persons *in* the economy, it is important to observe that they do not merely speak *of* the economy. The focus in each of the above instances is the *relation* that obtains *between* the persons, whether prior to or within the economy of redemption. Moreover, the fact that the New Testament portrays the missions of the Son and the Spirit as the means of unveiling God's true name and nature (Matt 11:25–27; John 17:3, 6) suggests that we should not draw too sharp a division between God's eternal modes of being and his temporal modes of operation. The distinction between the immanent Trinity and the economic Trinity does not map onto the Kantian distinction between noumenal and phenomenal realms. Better, I think, to see the temporal missions of the Son and the Spirit as the free, gracious, temporal extensions of their eternal, necessary, natural relations of origin.[51]

What about Warfield's worry that the traditional interpretation of the personal names compromises the full equality of the divine persons? The preceding discussion suggests that Warfield's worry is unjustified. According to the pattern of personal naming traced above, the eternal relations of origin that constitute the Son and the Spirit as divine persons do not constitute them as derivative deities. The eternal relations of origin that constitute the Son and the Spirit as divine persons are the bases of their full

---

51. On the relationship between eternal relations of origin and temporal missions, see Gilles Emery, *The Trinitarian Theology of Saint Thomas Aquinas*, trans. Francesca Aran Murphy (Oxford: Oxford University Press, 2007), chapter 15; Fred Sanders, *The Triune God*, New Studies in Dogmatics (Grand Rapids: Zondervan Academic, 2016), chapters 3–6. On the metaphysical distinctions involved in this relationship, see Scott R. Swain, *The God of the Gospel: Robert Jenson's Trinitarian Theology*, Strategic Initiatives in Evangelical Theology (Downers Grove, IL: IVP Academic, 2013), chapters 6–9.

ontological equality with the Father: the Son *of* God *is* God; the Spirit *of* God *is* God.[52] Moreover, this pattern of personal naming suggests that, far from undermining God's aseity, the doctrines of the eternal generation of the Son and the eternal procession of the Spirit actually deepen our understanding of God's perfection. Aseity is not merely a negative attribute, referring to God's lack of dependence on creatures. Aseity is a positive attribute, referring to the internal, tripersonal fecundity of God's life as Father, Son, and Spirit. God is eternally, internally full. And God's eternal, internal fullness is manifest in the eternal generation of the Son and the eternal procession of the Spirit.[53] As Warfield's European counterpart Herman Bavinck eloquently affirms, God's intra-Trinitarian fecundity "is a beautiful theme," which illumines both God's internal perfection as Father, Son, and Spirit and also God's external works:

> God is no abstract, fixed, monadic, solitary substance, but a plenitude of life. It is his nature (οὐσια) to be generative (γεννητικη) and fruitful (καρπογονος). It is capable of expansion, unfolding, communication. Those who deny

52. From a linguistic perspective, relations of origin (that is, eternal generation, eternal procession) gloss the personal names (that is, Son of God, Spirit of God). From a metaphysical perspective, relations of origin distinguish the persons without dividing the essence—indeed, they are the *only* way of distinguishing the persons without dividing the essence. Grasping this point helps us appreciate where uses of terms such as "subordination" are appropriate or inappropriate in Trinitarian theology. When the term "subordination" is used, as it traditionally has been used, to refer to relations of origin (or to their temporal expressions in mission), then the term is licit. When the term "subordination" is used, as it more recently has been used, as an alternative to relations of origin in order to distinguish the persons by relations of authority and submission, then the term is illicit. Whereas the former usage preserves what is common to the three (being, authority, glory, operation, etc.), the latter compromises what is common to the three, turning, for example, "authority" into a personal property of the Father rather than a common property of the three. In theological grammar, it is not the "lexicon" alone (that is, terminology) that determines whether a theological viewpoint is licit, but also the "syntax" (that is, ruled usage of terminology). See footnote 15 above.

53. Thomas Aquinas, *Summa Theologiae* I, q. 27, art. 5, ad 3; I, q. 32, art. 2, ad 3. For discussion of this theme in certain pro-Nicene fathers, see Anatolios, *Retrieving Nicaea*, 114–15, 190. It is worth noting here that linking personal generation with ontological subordination was a typically "Arian" theological move.

> this fecund productivity fail to take seriously the fact that God is an infinite fullness of blessed life. All such people have left is an abstract deistic concept of God, or to compensate for his sterility, in pantheistic fashion they include the life of the world in the divine being. Apart from the Trinity even the act of creation becomes inconceivable. For if God cannot communicate himself, he is a darkened light, a dry spring, unable to exert himself outward to communicate himself to creatures.[54]

THE PERSONAL PROPERTIES OF PATERNITY, FILIATION, AND SPIRATION

I conclude with several observations regarding the importance of the traditional rendering of the revealed names Father, Son, and Spirit by the personal properties of paternity, filiation, and spiration. First, the traditional interpretation suggests a *reason* for the Bible's employment of *these names in particular* in the revelation of the Triune God. The traditional interpretation claims that the Bible *calls* God "Father," "Son," and "Spirit" because relations of paternity, filiation, and spiration *exist* preeminently in God, in a sublime manner that ultimately transcends our understanding and evokes wonder. However, Warfield's interpretation, which reduces the meaning of "Son" to "likeness," cannot tell us why the Bible calls the second person of the Trinity God's "Son" rather than God's "Brother."[55] It is unclear, on Warfield's interpretation, what the personal names Father, Son, and Spirit actually *reveal* about the nature of God other than bare Triunity.

---

54. Herman Bavinck, *Reformed Dogmatics*, vol. 2, *God and Creation*, ed. John Bolt, trans. John Vriend (Grand Rapids: Baker Academic, 2004), 308–9.

55. Petrus van Mastricht makes a similar argument against critics of the doctrine of eternal generation like Röell. See Mastricht, *Theoretical-Practical Theology* (Grand Rapids: Reformation Heritage Books, 2019), 2:556.

Second, the traditional interpretation of the personal names of the Trinity is hermeneutically productive. Among other things, Wesley Hill's book *Paul and the Trinity* demonstrates how classical categories of "persons in (asymmetrical) relations" help us move beyond the constraints of the modern interpretive categories of "high" and "low" Christologies, providing a richer, more nuanced reading of Pauline texts.[56] Elsewhere, Andreas Köstenberger and I have attempted to demonstrate the profitability of these categories for interpreting the Gospel of John.[57]

Third, the traditional interpretation offers a way of relating and distinguishing God's eternal modes of being and his temporal modes of operation. It is one of the stranger ironies of modern Reformed and evangelical theology that many who follow Warfield in rejecting the eternal generation of the Son have seized on eternal subordination—a notion fiercely opposed by Warfield—as the distinctive personal property of the Son.[58] The traditional interpretation of the personal names of the Trinity allows us to honor Warfield's insight that the obedience of the incarnate Son is a contingent consequence of the intra-Trinitarian covenant of redemption, not a necessary feature of his personal identity, all the while showing us how the Son's economic obedience reflects his eternal generation from the Father.[59]

Fourth, the traditional interpretation of the personal names of the Trinity helps us better appreciate the soteriological and

---

56. Wesley Hill, *Paul and the Trinity: Persons, Relations, and the Pauline Letters* (Grand Rapids: Eerdmans, 2015).

57. Andreas J. Köstenberger and Scott R. Swain, *Father, Son and Spirit: The Trinity and John's Gospel*, New Studies in Biblical Theology (Downers Grove, IL: InterVarsity Press, 2008), especially chapters 7–8, and 10.

58. See, most recently, many of the essays in Bruce A. Ware and John Starke, ed., *One God in Three Persons: Unity of Essence, Distinction of Persons, Implications for Life* (Wheaton: Crossway, 2015). See also footnote 52 above.

59. For further development of this theme, see Scott R. Swain and Michael Allen, "The Obedience of the Eternal Son," *IJST* 15 (2013): 114–34; Thomas Joseph White, *The Incarnate Lord: A Thomistic Study in Christology* (Washington, DC: Catholic University of America Press, 2015), chapter 6.

religious significance of Trinitarian theology. One of the great strengths of Warfield's *ISBE* article is its focus on the soteriological and religious setting of New Testament teaching on the Trinity. Warfield states,

> If he [the Christian] could not construct the doctrine of the Trinity out of his consciousness of salvation, yet the elements of his consciousness of salvation are interpreted to him and reduced to order only by the doctrine of the Trinity which he finds underlying and giving their significance and consistency to the teaching of the Scriptures as to the process of salvation. By means of this doctrine he is able to think clearly and consequently of his threefold relation to the saving God, experienced by him as Fatherly love sending a Redeemer, as redeeming love executing redemption, as saving love applying redemption: all manifestations in distinct methods and by distinct agencies of the one seeking and saving love of God.[60]

The personal properties of paternity, filiation, and spiration further enrich and expand our understanding and experience of this "one seeking and saving love of God." How so? They help us see that the eternal covenant of redemption—the foundation of all God's saving works in time—flows from and expresses the deep, mutual, and eternal delight of the blessed Trinity. They help us see that the Father who has eternally begotten an eternally beloved Son also wills to bring many other sons to glory. They help us see that, at the Father's sovereign behest, the Father's only-begotten Son has willed to become our kinsman redeemer, assuming our creaturely nature and satisfying our twofold debt to God's law, in order that he might become the firstborn among many redeemed brothers and sisters. They help us see that the Holy

60. Warfield, "Trinity," 3021.

Spirit, who eternally proceeds in the mutual love of the Father and the Son, has equipped the Son with all things necessary for redeeming his brothers and sisters; and, that redemption being accomplished, the Spirit now applies the blessings of adoption to us, uniting us to our incarnate elder brother and welcoming us into the fellowship which the Spirit has enjoyed with the Father and the Son from eternity and which we, in, with, and by the blessed Trinity, will enjoy for eternity as well, to the eternal praise of our great God and Savior: the Father, the Son, and the Holy Spirit.

GOD'S LORDLY SON

MARK 12:35–37 AND TRINITARIAN CHRISTOLOGY[1]

The purpose of the present essay is to reflect theologically on the riddle posed by Jesus in Mark 12:35–37, the so-called *Davidssohnfrage*—that is, the question regarding David's son. The goal is to demonstrate the way in which this text contributes to Mark's Trinitarian Christology: namely, his claim that the Messiah is "one of the Trinity" (*unus ex Trinitate*), God's lordly Son. Before discussing this passage, however, a few words regarding the nature of theological commentary in general, and regarding the theological interpretation of the Gospels in particular, are in order.

ON THEOLOGICAL COMMENTARY

Theological commentary is a human activity ordered by and to the knowledge of the Triune God. As such, it is bound and shaped by realities common to every dimension of the knowledge

1. The present essay is published in a Festschrift for Henri Blocher edited by Michael Allen, *Theological Commentary* (London: T&T Clark, 2011). It was a great pleasure to participate in this tribute to Henri Blocher. Few have labored as a "scribe who has been trained for the kingdom" (Matt 13:52) with the fidelity, wisdom, and excellence of Professor Blocher. May God continue to grant such gifts to the church.

of God.[2] The possibility of theological knowledge is grounded ontologically in the intra-Trinitarian knowledge and love of God himself. "No one knows the Son except the Father, and no one knows the Father except the Son" (Matt 11:27). The possibility of theological knowledge is grounded epistemologically in the fact that God, in his sovereign good pleasure, has condescended to reveal himself to babes (11:25–26). "No one knows the Father except the Son and anyone to whom the Son chooses to reveal him" (11:27).[3]

To know and adore the blessed Trinity is not our possession by natural right. Here we are dealing with a knowledge that is natural only to God, a knowledge that is ours therefore only because God has freely "granted" us to know "the mystery of the kingdom of God" (Mark 4:11 KJV). In acquiring this knowledge, we are like the one in Matthew 13:44 who stumbles on a treasure hidden in a field. We did not mean to find it. Our possession of this treasure is not the conclusion to our skillful quest. Nevertheless, though the finding of this treasure does not result from our intelligent action, its finding does result in manifold forms of intelligent activity. The lucky day laborer of Matthew 13:44 becomes the skillful scribe and wise householder of Matthew 13:52. The gift of theological knowledge awakens and energizes the work of theological reason. This work of theological reason, like all regenerated energies, is in turn a work characterized by mortification and vivification. In terms of mortification: There is a selling of all that we have to lay hold of this hidden treasure—a kind of intellectual and affective divestment, an ascesis—that follows from our finding this gift. We do not know God. But, in God's kindness, we have come to know him.

---

2. Geerhardus Vos, "The Idea of Biblical Theology as a Science and as a Theological Discipline," in *Redemptive History and Biblical Interpretation*, ed. Richard B. Gaffin Jr. (Phillipsburg, NJ: Presbyterian & Reformed, 1980), 4.

3. For a recent reflection on theology's twin *principia*, see John Webster, "Principles of Systematic Theology," *IJST* 11 (2009): 56–71.

And therefore we forsake all that we think we know in order more fully to know him. In terms of vivification: There is a new manner of "mindfulness" that corresponds to the riches freely received.[4] This new mindfulness is characterized by confidence, corresponding to the promise of divine assistance that accompanies our study: "Consider what I say, for the Lord will give you understanding in everything" (2 Tim 2:7 NASB). It is also characterized by a holy diligence, corresponding to the gravitas of our study's object and end.[5] Moreover, as is the case with every labor carried out under the banner of the risen Christ (1 Cor 15:58), this work is characterized by joy: "I rejoice at your word like one who finds great spoil" (Ps 119:162).[6]

As a mode of theological reasoning, theological commentary concerns itself directly and specifically with the textual mediation of God's self-revelation in the sacred writings of his authorized emissaries: the prophets and the apostles. The concern here is not simply the sacred writings taken as a whole, as in dogmatics, but the sacred writings in their distinctive portions and places (see Heb 1:1). Theological commentary is that branch of theological reasoning that attends to the *specific* words of Isaiah, Mark, or Paul. Holy Scripture affords us with an embarrassment of riches, and we are concerned to identify and appreciate each treasure of holy Scripture in its distinctive beauty and worth.

Theological commentary thus devotes its attention to the particular words of a particular scriptural text or book in its particular historical and literary setting in order to provide a faithful representation of its particular message. This attentiveness to particularity is preserved from myopia and atomism because it attends to the various *words* of holy Scripture under the promise of finding *the Word made flesh* therein. "If anyone ... reads

4. Desmond, *God and the Between* (see 16n30).

5. John Chrysostom, *Homilies on Matthew* 1.17.

6. Karl Barth, *Evangelical Theology: An Introduction*, trans. Grover Foley (Grand Rapids: Eerdmans, 1963), 155–56.

the Scriptures with attention," Irenaeus assures us, "he will find in them an account of Christ, and a foreshadowing of the new calling. For Christ is the treasure which was hid in the field."[7]

Here we must emphasize that the principle of scriptural unity is not simply a literary hypothesis that the commentator, as rational subject, brings to the text, which is his object. The Word made flesh is the lively subject of scriptural revelation[8] who communicates himself in and through the words of his Spirit-inspired ambassadors, thus enabling us to appreciate their fundamental unity and coherence in him (Luke 24:44–47; 1 Pet 1:11; Rom 10:17). Reading is therefore a living *conversation* between an eloquent Lord and his attentive servants, a conversation in which the reader is summoned to hear what the Spirit of Christ *says* to the churches (Rev 2:7). Answering this summons, theological commentary is the work of scribes "trained for the kingdom of heaven" (Matt 13:52), who labor diligently in the field of the Word's self-communication and who, like wise householders, freely distribute the fruits of their labors, "both enriching the understanding of men, and showing forth the wisdom of God."[9] Such labor is both pleasing to God (2 Tim 2:15) and (quite literally) salutary in its ends (1 Tim 4:13–16). Such labor therefore requires no further warrant.

The four Gospels play a distinctive role in the unfolding economy of God's self-revelation, and we must be aware of this role if we are to read them responsibly. The Gospels announce the historical realization and revelation of "the mystery of the kingdom of God" (Mark 4:11 KJV). According to the four evangelists, God has exercised his "kingly self-assertion"[10] in accom-

---

7. Irenaeus, *Against Heresies*, in *The Ante-Nicene Fathers*, ed. Alexander Roberts and James Donaldson, 10 vols. (1885–1887; repr., Peabody, MA: Hendrickson, 1994), 4.26.1.

8. See Vos, "Idea," 4–5.

9. Irenaeus, *Against Heresies* 4.26.1.

10. Herman Ridderbos, *The Coming of the Kingdom*, trans. H. de Jongste (Philadelphia: Presbyterian & Reformed, 1962), 19.

plishing the salvation long promised in Israel's scriptures. In doing so, he has unveiled secrets "hidden from the foundation of the world" (Matt 13:35). Central to these accounts of the kingdom's realization and revelation is the figure of Jesus, God's anointed Son. The unveiling of God's saving kingship thus comes in and through the unveiling of Jesus' identity and mission. And so, while the Gospels include instruction about eschatology, the church, salvation, politics, and discipleship, they are primarily "*about Christ*, telling who he is, what he did, said, and suffered."[11] The chief aim of the evangelists, says Calvin, is to "place before our eyes" the "Christ who has been sent by the Father, that our faith may acknowledge him to be the Author of a blessed life."[12]

The literary form of the Gospels corresponds to the historical form of the kingdom's fulfillment in Jesus. Because the Gospels tell us who Jesus is and what he did, said, and suffered, their message is rendered in the form of "a chronicle, a story, a narrative."[13] The Gospels are narrative Christologies. As is characteristic of their narrative form, the Gospels' material claims are more often rendered indirectly than directly. Like their Old Testament narrative counterparts, the Gospel narratives do not "sermonize."[14] They prefer to show their doctrine rather than to tell it.[15]

Moreover, because these messianic narratives concern the historical realization and revelation of a *mystery*, we find

---

11. Martin Luther, "A Brief Instruction on What to Look for and Expect in the Gospels," in *Martin Luther's Basic Theological Writings*, ed. Timothy F. Lull (Minneapolis: Fortress, 1989), 105 (emphasis mine).

12. John Calvin, *Commentary on a Harmony of the Evangelists, Matthew, Mark, and Luke*, Calvin's Commentaries 16. trans. William Pringle (repr., Grand Rapids: Baker, 1998), xxxvii.

13. Luther, "Brief Instruction," 105.

14. J. P. Fokkelman, *Reading Biblical Narrative: An Introductory Guide* (Louisville: Westminster John Knox, 1999), 149.

15. Mark Allan Powell, *What Is Narrative Criticism?* (Minneapolis: Fortress, 1990), 52.

ourselves confronted with parables, riddles, and enigmas on almost every page. The enigmatic forms of these writings repeatedly threaten to confound us even as they promise to communicate and to console. This feature of the evangelical histories should not be taken as evidence of christological ambiguity on the part of the evangelists, however. The Gospels are *revelations* not perpetuations of the mystery. Consequently, they intend to evoke a quite definite confession on the part of the reader (see Mark 15:39; John 20:28, 31). Nor is the more reticent form of the evangelists' claims evidence of an early stage in the evolution of christological reflection. The Ritschlian-Harnackian narrative of dogmatic development long ago wore out its promise as a hermeneutical lens for interpreting these texts. (Let the reader understand!) The indirect nature of the evangelists' *modus loquendi* is neither a sign of theological ambiguity nor of theological primitiveness. Rather, the literary form of the Gospel records corresponds to their appointment to serve the mystery of God's kingship, which is realized *sub contrario*. God's revelation is realized through his hiddenness, God's salvation through his judgment, God's kingly reign through his humble service (see Mark 10:45).[16] Accordingly, it belongs to the reader of the Gospels not only to follow them *to the place* they wish to lead us—to the knowledge of the Triune God and to eternal life (John 17:3)—but also to follow them *on the path* they wish to lead us if we are to receive their gift and understand their message.

TRANSLATION

> And while he was teaching in the temple, Jesus answered[17] and said, "How can the scribes say that the Messiah is the son of David? David himself declared in the Holy Spirit,

---

16. Compare with Ridderbos, who speaks of "the specific modality of the revelation of the kingdom of heaven" (*Coming*, 123–29).

17. Although ἀποκριθεὶς is often left untranslated, I have translated it because it seems to fulfill a similar function to that of the other participle in this verse (διδάσκων)—that is,

> 'The Lord said to my Lord, Sit at my right hand, until I put your enemies under your feet.' David himself calls him Lord; so how is he his son?" And the great crowd heard him gladly.

SETTING

Our text appears in the middle of the last major section of Mark's Gospel (11:1–13:37) before the passion narrative (14:1–15:47).[18] The events of 12:35–37 transpire on the last day of Jesus' three day sojourn in the temple and its environs, on Tuesday of Mark's "holy week."[19] Verse 35 relates the immediate setting of these events as occurring διδάσκων ἐν τῷ ἱερῷ, "while he was teaching in the temple." Mark 12:13–34 has been characterized as "Jesus' Jerusalem *didachē*."[20] This characterization nicely captures not only the events of 12:13–34 but also those of 12:1–40 in their entirety. The focus in this subsection is on Jesus' status as messianic teacher.[21]

Jesus' Jerusalem teaching occurs in the context of increasingly heightened conflict with the authoritative teachers of

---

that of providing the setting for Jesus' question (see "Setting," below).

18. See Joel Marcus's outline, *Mark 1–8: A New Translation with Introduction and Commentary*, AB 27 (New Haven: Yale University Press, 2002), 64.

19. Joel Marcus, *Mark 8–16: A New Translation with Introduction and Commentary*, AB 27a (New Haven: Yale University Press, 2009), 767–79. For a brief but helpful discussion of Mark's account in relation to those of the other evangelists, see Robert H. Stein, *Mark*, Baker Exegetical Commentary on the New Testament (Grand Rapids: Baker Academic, 2008), 499–502. Concerning Mark's "Holy Week," Stein concludes, "Whether Mark intended his readers to understand all of 11.1–16.8 as taking place within this tight chronological framework is unlikely" (499). Stein then cites "the famous quotation of Papias," which says, "Mark ... wrote accurately all that he remembered, not, indeed, in order, of the things said or done by the Lord (Eusebius, *Eccl. Hist.* 3.39.15)" (499n1).

20. John R. Donahue, "A Neglected Factor in the Theology of Mark," *JBL* 101 (1982): 570.

21. Some form of διδάσκω or διδάσκαλος appears five times in 12:1–40 with reference to Jesus, representing a little over 20 percent of their occurrences in Mark's Gospel. Other words and phrases in these verses also emphasize Jesus' status as teacher, including "speaking in parables" in 12:1 and "answering" in 12:28, 29, 35. On the theme of Jesus as messianic teacher in Mark, see Adela Yarbro Collins, *Mark: A Commentary*, Hermeneia (Minneapolis: Fortress, 2007), 73–79.

Israel.[22] Though their opposition to his ministry has been apparent from the beginning (for example, 2:6–7, 16, 24; 3:2, 6), it is now growing stronger. As Jesus predicted (8:31), the time of the Son of Man's rejection has come (compare 12:10).[23] Furthermore, the conflict between Jesus and Israel's teachers is now unfolding on the latter's home turf, the temple.[24] Mark 12:1–40 presents Jesus' extended response to the challenge to his authority raised by "the chief priests, the scribes, and the elders" (11:27–28) on the heels of his astonishing words and actions in the temple on the previous day (11:12–19).[25] The function of 12:1–40 in this regard explains the presence of ἀποκριθεὶς in 12:35. Jesus' riddle in 12:35–37 represents his last public "answer" to the question concerning his authority before his trial.

The themes of Jesus' teaching in the temple include his authority to act as God's agent (12:1–12, 35–37) as well as his authority as an interpreter of Israel's scriptures (especially 12:18–34) (see "Structure" below). The last question asked of Jesus in this subsection measures his orthodoxy by the standard of what his contemporaries understood to be the first principle of scriptural teaching: the requirement to acknowledge and honor the one true and living God (12:28–34; compare Philo, *On the Decalogue* 65; Josephus, *Jewish Antiquities* 3.91).[26] Jesus' answer reveals his (and the evangelist's) firm commitment to

---

22. Those engaging Jesus in 12:1–40 include the scribes, the Pharisees, the Herodians, and the Sadducees (see 12:13, 18, 28, 35, 38).

23. A form of ἀποδοκιμάζω is used in both 8:31 and 12:10, thus linking Jesus' prediction regarding his rejection with the events described in the parable.

24. Compare Josephus's characterization of the experts in the law as "scribes of the temple" (*Jewish Antiquities* 12.142). See also Collins, *Mark*, 73.

25. So Joanna Dewey, *Markan Public Debate: Literary Technique, Concentric Structure, and Theology in Mark 2:1–3:6*, SBL Dissertation Series 48 (Chico, CA: Scholars Press, 1980), 164–65.

26. As Jerome Neyrey observes, the theme of "giving God his due" pervades 12:13–34 (*Render to God: New Testament Understandings of the Divine* [Minneapolis: Fortress, 2004], 16–17). Donahue notes with respect to 12:13–34 that "*theos* is used 13 times in 21 verses, the most intense concentration in the gospel" ("Neglected Factor," 570n21).

Jewish monotheism, as he provides the New Testament's only direct quotation of Deuteronomy 6:4 (Mark 12:39–40; compare 10:18).[27] Jesus' rhetorical question for the scribes in turn concerns whether they have sufficiently acknowledged the lordly status of God's messianic King, in accordance with the divine revelation given through David in Psalm 110 (Mark 12:35–37). Have they respected God's beloved Son (12:6)? The subsection of Mark 12:1–40 concludes in verses 38–40 with a warning against the spiritual vices that will keep readers of sacred Scripture from acknowledging this scripturally promised divine Son and thus from entering into the kingdom of God (12:38–40; compare 12:7).

STRUCTURE

Mark 12:1–40 and 12:35–37 exhibit symmetrical patterns. In 12:1–40, Jesus responds to questions regarding his authority (compare 11:28) in two fundamental ways.[28] The first type of response is found in verses 1–12 (A) and verses 35–40 (A'). It takes an antagonistic stance toward the Jewish leaders and addresses Jesus' authority as God's beloved/lordly Son, coupled with a warning against those who reject him. The second type of response—in verses 13–17 (B), verses 18–27 (C), and verses 28–34 (B')—takes a more affirmative stance toward the Jewish leaders, or at least toward the teaching of the Pharisees, and displays Jesus' commitment to some of biblical Judaism's most basic beliefs. In 12:35–37, the structural emphasis falls on the citation of Psalm 110:1, which serves as inspired evidence of the Messiah's lordly status and therefore as the basis for rebuking the scribes' failure to appreciate what David "in the Holy Spirit" declared.

---

27. M. Eugene Boring, "Markan Christology: God-Language for Jesus?," *NTS* 45 (1999): 456.

28. Compare Dewey, *Markan Public*, 162–63.

An outline of Mark 12:1–40[29]

A	vv. 1–12	The authority of God's beloved Son plus a threat of divine judgment
B	vv. 13–17	Giving God his due: money
C	vv. 18–27	God's power to raise the dead
B'	vv. 28–34	Giving God his due: the love of God and neighbor
A'	vv. 35–40	The authority of God's lordly Son plus a threat of divine judgment

An outline of Mark 12:35–37[30]

A And while he was teaching in the temple, Jesus answered and said,

B "How can the scribes say that the Messiah is the son of David?

C David himself, in the Holy Spirit, declared,

D 'The Lord said to my Lord, Sit at my right hand, until I put your enemies under your feet.'

C' David himself calls him Lord;

B' so how is he his son?"

A' And the great crowd heard him gladly.

COMMENTARY

Having responded to three questions from his opponents (Mark 12:13–34), Jesus now responds with a question of his own. The question concerns the filial descent of the Messiah. At issue is the view of the scribes, who say the Messiah is David's

29. Compare with the more extended outline of Dewey, *Markan Public Debate*, 162.

30. Here I follow Joel Marcus, *The Way of the Lord: Christological Exegesis of the Old Testament in the Gospel of Mark* (Louisville: Westminster John Knox, 1992), 130–31.

son, versus the view uttered prophetically by David himself, who calls the Messiah his Lord. Though Jesus' understanding of the Messiah's pedigree remains implicit in this passage, the immediate context (12:1–12), as well as the context of the Mark's Gospel as a whole, makes the point clearly. The Messiah is not merely David's son. He is God's lordly Son, sent into the world to inaugurate God's long-awaited kingdom and destined to share in God's kingly glory.

"And while he was teaching in the temple, Jesus answered and said." As discussed previously (see "Setting" and "Structure," above), the two participles in 12:35 (ἀποκριθεὶς and διδάσκων) provide the setting for Jesus' question concerning the Messiah's descent. The chief priests, the scribes, and the elders have questioned Jesus' authority to speak and act as he did in the temple on the previous day (11:27–28), and Jesus has already addressed this question indirectly in two ways: first with a question about the source of John the Baptist's authority (11:29–30), and then with a parable regarding "a beloved son" (12:1–12). He has also vindicated himself as an authoritative teacher of Israel's scriptures by showing his commitment to giving the one Lord God his due. According to Jesus, Caesar deserves what belongs to him and God deserves what belongs to him (12:13–17), including the acknowledgment of his power to raise the dead (12:18–27) and his identity as the one true and living God (12:28–34).[31] Jesus now addresses the question about his authority one last time by posing a conundrum regarding the Messiah's filial descent: "How can the scribes say that the Messiah is the son of David?"

The belief that the Messiah would be of Davidic stock was commonplace by the time of the New Testament. This belief was rooted in a host of Old Testament Scriptures (for example, 2 Sam 7:12–16; Isa 11:1; Jer 23:5–6) and reflected in other

31. Neyrey, *Render to God*, 18–19.

Jewish writings as well (for example, Psalms of Solomon 17.21; 4QFlorilegium [174] I, 7–19).[32] According to some interpreters, Jesus' question is designed to sever the link between the Messiah and David in one of two ways. His question is taken either as an affirmation of his own messianic status while denying his Davidic lineage[33] or, from the opposite side, as an affirmation of his Davidic lineage while denying his messianic status.[34] Both interpretations fail, however, not only because they do not fit Mark's overarching characterization of Jesus as both Messiah and son of David (for example, 1:1; 8:29; 10:47–48; 11:10; 14:61–62),[35] but also because they do not appreciate how questions function in Markan discourse more broadly and in this text more specifically.[36] In certain key examples related to the issue of his identity in the latter half of Mark's Gospel, Jesus' questions are not designed to reject categorically the position held by his interlocutors, but to demonstrate the position's insufficiency taken on its own. Jesus' question in 8:29 is not meant to deny his prophetic vocation (compare 6:4).[37] Nor is his question in 10:18 meant to deny his status as "Good Teacher."[38] As the preceding

---

32. See Christopher Burger, *Jesus als Davidssohn: Eine traditionsgeschichtliche Untersuchung* (Göttingen: Vandenhoeck & Ruprecht, 1970), 16–24, and the literature cited therein.

33. Paul J. Achtemeier, "'And He Followed Him': Miracles and Discipleship in Mark 10:46–52," *Semeia* 11 (1978): 115–45; followed recently by Elizabeth Struthers Malbon, *Mark's Jesus: Characterization as Narrative Christology* (Waco: Baylor University Press, 2009), 159. Malbon considers this interpretation to be the "obvious conclusion."

34. Bruce D. Chilton, "Jesus ben David: Reflections on the *Davidssohnfrage*," *JSNT* 14 (1982): 88–112.

35. For an extended argument in this regard, see Burger, *Jesus als Davidssohn*, 42–71.

36. For a helpful discussion of the role of questions in Mark's Gospel, see Robert M. Fowler, *Let the Reader Understand: Reader-Response Criticism and the Gospel of Mark* (Minneapolis: Fortress, 1991), 131–34. According to Fowler's count, "there are 114 questions in Mark's Gospel, 77 of them unanswered" (132n8).

37. See Marcus, *Mark 8–16*, 611, who, following Räisänen, describes Jesus' question as "Socratic."

38. See Joel Marcus, "Authority to Forgive Sins upon the Earth: The *Shema* in the Gospel of Mark," in *The Gospels and the Scriptures of Israel*, ed. Craig A. Evans and W. Richard Stegner (Sheffield: Sheffield Academic, 1994), 208–10.

examples suggest, Jesus' questions often function to accomplish rhetorically what his two-stage healing of the blind man in 8:22–26 accomplished symbolically, that of moving someone from partial to fuller vision.[39] In the present text, then, the point of Jesus' question seems to be that the Messiah is "more than David's son."[40]

Robert Gundry presents a unique variation on the interpretation that Jesus is denying the Messiah's Davidic descent. He understands Jesus to be inquiring after the scriptural source of the (mistaken) scribal belief that the Messiah would be a son of David.[41] This interpretation rests, however, on too narrow an understanding of πόθεν in 12:37, which can mean not only "whence" in terms of *location* but also "whence" in terms of *origin* and of *cause* (as in, "How can it be?").[42] Moreover, Gundry's interpretation saddles Jesus with exactly the sort of hermeneutical narrowness that he has just rebuked in the Sadducees in 12:18–27. Surely Jesus does not require the Sadducees to make good and necessary inferences from scriptural premises in one moment only to rebuke the scribes for doing so in the next! Jesus' question is not intended to deny the Davidic descent of the Messiah or to challenge the scriptural foundations for this belief. His concern is to question the adequacy of this belief as an explanation of the Messiah's identity and authority.

---

39. As Fowler puts it, "questions sow seeds of thought" (*Let the Reader Understand*, 132).

40. Burger, *Jesus als Davidssohn*, 66; see also 168–69. Marcus takes an interesting approach to this text, suggesting that Mark 12:35–37 in its immediate context denies the Messiah's Davidic sonship but that in its broader Markan context only serves to qualify the adequacy of the Messiah's Davidic sonship as an explanation of his identity: "Jesus is *not (just)* the Son of David *but (also)* the Son of God" ("Identity and Ambiguity in Markan Christology," in *Seeking the Identity of Jesus: A Pilgrimage*, ed. Beverly Roberts Gaventa and Richard B. Hays [Grand Rapids: Eerdmans, 2008], 139–40, emphasis original).

41. Robert H. Gundry, *Mark: A Commentary on His Apology for the Cross* (Grand Rapids: Eerdmans, 1993), 718–19, 722–23.

42. Henry George Liddell, Robert Scott, and Henry Stuart Jones, *A Greek-English Lexicon*, 9th ed. with a revised supplement (Oxford: Clarendon, 1996), s.v.

In order to demonstrate the inadequacy of the scribal perspective, Jesus cites what David himself declared about the matter in Psalm 110:1: "The Lord said to my Lord, Sit at my right hand, until I put your enemies under your feet." The authority of David's perspective lies in the fact that he speaks *in the Holy Spirit*. The use of similar language elsewhere suggests a visionary experience (Ezek 11:24; 37:1; Rev 1:10; 4:2; 17:3; 21:10) or prophetic utterance (Neh 9:30; Mic 3:8; Zech 7:12) enabled by the Holy Spirit.[43] David's perspective on the matter thus represents God's perspective on the matter.

Mark's citation of Psalm 110:1 follows the Septuagint of Psalm 109:1 with two exceptions. Mark lacks the article before κύριος and has ὑποκάτω instead of ὑποπόδιον (compare Matt 22:44).[44] The latter discrepancy likely signals a conflation of Psalm 110:1 and Psalm 8:6 (8:7 LXX), a conflation present in other New Testament writings as well (1 Cor 15:25–27; Eph 1:20–22; Heb 1:13–2:8).[45] This conflation in turn suggests that Mark may be drawing his citation from a messianic *testimonium*, a collection of Old Testament prooftexts related to the Messiah.[46] Whatever Mark's relation to the Septuagint and to these possible collections may be, it is clear that he wishes to trace the use of one of early Christianity's most important messianic prooftexts back to Jesus himself. The question is, why? What role does Psalm 110:1 play in the present context?

---

43. The examples cited have ἐν πνεύματι instead of ἐν τῷ πνεύματι, as we have it in 12:36. The meaning, nevertheless, seems to be equivalent.

44. For a discussion of the various text forms of Ps 110:1 that are cited in the New Testament, see David M. Hay, *Glory at the Right Hand: Psalm 110 and Early Christianity* (Nashville: Abingdon, 1973), 34–38.

45. On the theological significance of this conflation, see Martin Hengel, "Sit at My Right Hand," in *Studies in Early Christology* (Edinburgh: T&T Clark, 1995), 163–72.

46. See Martin C. Albl, *"And Scripture Cannot Be Broken": The Form and Function of the Early Christian* Testimonia *Collections* (Leiden: Brill, 1999), 222–28, 236.

Psalm 110 seems to have played little to no role in the messianic expectation of pre-Christian Judaism.[47] However, it takes on a dramatic new role in early Christianity, becoming the most commonly cited Old Testament messianic prooftext in the New Testament[48] and providing the exegetical foundation for a host of christological topics treated in both the New Testament and beyond.[49] According to early Christian writers, Psalm 110 predicts the Messiah's heavenly vindication, glory, and enthronement (Matt 26:64; Acts 2:33–36; Eph 1:20–23; Heb 1:3–4, 13–14; etc.),

---

47. Hengel, "Sit at My Right Hand," 179. Hengel suggests that Psalm 110 influenced the Similitudes of 1 Enoch ("Sit at My Right Hand," 185–89). However, Richard Bauckham argues against such an influence, noting the lack of direct allusion to the text (Bauckham, "The Throne of God and the Worship of Jesus," in *The Jewish Roots of Christological Monotheism: Papers from the St. Andrews Conference on the Historical Origins of the Worship of Jesus*, ed. Carey C. Newman, James R. Davila, and Gladys S. Lewis, Supplements to the Journal for the Study of Judaism [Leiden: Brill, 1999], 57–60). On the basis of the common themes that appear in 11QMelchizedek and Psalm 110, Marcus argues that the former "should be considered a chapter in the history of the interpretation of Ps. 110" (*Way*, 133; similarly, Hengel, "Sit at My Right Hand," 182). However, the themes Marcus identifies are common to a host of Old Testament eschatological texts. Furthermore, as John J. Collins notes, our fragments of 11QMelchizedek do not contain any direct verbal allusions to Psalm 110 (John J. Collins, *The Scepter and the Star: The Messiahs of the Dead Sea Scrolls and Other Ancient Literature* [New York: Doubleday, 1995], 142). Testament of Job 33.3 does speak of Job's throne at God's right hand, and thus undoubtedly alludes to Psalm 110:1. However, Job is not cast in the role of God's eschatological agent/Messiah in this text. His enthronement instead seems to function as a reward for his piety (compare Bauckham, "Throne of God," 62n37), the latter being a common theme in pre-Christian Jewish literature (see Hay, *Glory*, 55). The most notable exception to the dearth of messianic reflection on Psalm 110 (also noted by Hengel, "Sit at My Right Hand," 179) lies in the canonical edition of the Psalter itself, where the exaltation of "my Lord" to God's right hand in Psalm 110 follows the psalmist's plea for deliverance from his adversaries in Psalm 109. See especially 109:26–31; verse 31 states that the Lord "stands at the right hand of the needy one, to save him from those who condemn his soul to death." This example is particularly interesting for the interpretation of Mark 12:36 because earlier in this subsection (12:10–11) the evangelist cites Psalm 118:22–23 as a prophecy of the Messiah's suffering and vindication.

48. Hay identifies 22 citations of or allusions to Psalm 110:1 in the New Testament: Matt 22:41–46; 26:64; Mark 12:35–37; 14:62; 16:19; Luke 20:41–44; 22:69; Acts 2:33–36; 5:31; 7:55–56; Rom 8:34; 1 Cor 15:25; Eph 1:20; 2:6; Col 3:1; Heb 1:3, 13; 8:1; 10:12–13; 12:2; 1 Pet 3:22; Rev 3:21 (*Glory*, 45–46). See also Hengel ("Sit at My Right Hand," 133) and Bauckham (*Jesus and the God of Israel: God Crucified and Other Studies on the New Testament's Christology of Divine Identity* [Grand Rapids: Eerdmans, 2008], 173), who identify 21 and 20 citations or allusions respectively.

49. For much of the following, see Hay, *Glory*, 45–51.

as well as his priestly ministry at the Father's right hand (Heb 5:10; 6:20; 7:21–28). It is also taken as evidence of the Messiah's eternal generation and divinity.[50] In our passage, Psalm 110:1 functions as a prophecy of the Messiah's vindication and glory, a prophecy that, as such, includes an implicit threat against his enemies.[51] In this regard, its function is very similar to that of Psalm 118:22–23 in Mark 12:10–11. However, the main function of this psalm lies in the inference that Jesus draws in verse 37 regarding the Messiah's sonship: "David himself calls him Lord; so how is he his son?"

The first part of the inference concerns the inadequacy of the scribal understanding of the Messiah's descent. The line of reasoning is this: because David calls the Messiah his "Lord," a merely Davidic understanding of the Messiah's ancestry is inadequate. The question for us concerns how this line of reasoning works. What is it about the servant/Lord relation between David and the Messiah that relativizes the father/son relation between David and the Messiah? The answer cannot be that "Lord" and "my Lord" are simply functioning here as honorific titles for the promised eschatological king. To be sure, both terms are commonly ascribed to anointed human kings in the Septuagint without any connotation of divinity whatsoever (see, for example, 1 Sam 26:18–19; 2 Sam 1:10; 3:21; 9:11; 11:11; 13:32, 33). Moreover, generally speaking, it would have sounded strange in the ancient world to hear a father call his son—"Lord."[52] However, in this instance, we are not talking about just any father or about just any son. We are talking about David, the recipient of covenant promises, and about the Messiah, the ultimate eschatological object of those promises. And if we consider this fact, it seems that no Second Temple Jew would have been surprised to hear David

50. Hay, *Glory*, 48–50.

51. So Marcus, *Way*, 134–37; and Rikk E. Watts, "Mark," in *Commentary on the New Testament Use of the Old Testament*, ed. G. K. Beale and D. A. Carson (Grand Rapids: Baker Academic, 2007), 222.

52. Marcus, *Mark*, 2:847.

call his promised son—*the* promised son, "Lord."[53] After all, the point of the Davidic covenant is that the One who will enjoy an everlasting throne, and thus an everlasting lordly status, is none other than the filial offspring of David (2 Sam 7:14, 16)! Therefore, it is not clear how interpreting "Lord" as merely an honorific title for the promised eschatological king accounts for the supposed inadequacy of the scribes' understanding.

In this passage, the significance of the title "Lord" does not lie primarily in the title itself. The significance lies in the place where the recipient of this title sits—on God's throne, at God's right hand. In Second Temple Judaism, God's heavenly throne serves as a symbol of his unique and unrivaled deity.[54] While Jews of this era know of many heavenly figures who enjoy an exalted status in God's presence, their exalted status is clearly distinguished from God's. Two examples are worth mentioning. In some texts these figures sit on thrones that are distinguished from God's throne (for example, 2 Enoch 20.1–3; Testament of Levi 3.8; Col 1:16). In other texts, they are depicted as standing in God's presence—that is, taking "the posture of servants" (for example, 2 Baruch 21.6; 4 Maccabees 17.18; Heb 1:13–14).[55] Both sorts of portrayals thus preserve, in different ways, the Jewish monotheistic belief in God's singular sovereignty. Consequently, for a figure to sit on God's own throne, as a handful of figures in pre-Christian Jewish literature do—including the Danielic Son of Man (Dan 7:9–14; 1 Enoch 45.3; 51.3; 69.27; 84.3), Wisdom (Wis 9:4), and the messianic King of Psalm 110—is for that figure to share in God's singular sovereignty and to exercise a prerogative that is uniquely

53. In the Psalms of Solomon, the coming "son of David" (17:21) is called "the Lord Messiah" (18:1).

54. See especially Bauckham, "Throne of God."

55. Bauckham, "Throne of God," 52–53. It is the latter stance, interestingly, that characterizes Metraton (who also, however, is enthroned) and Melchizedek, two of intertestamental Judaism's most exalted heavenly figures. See Hengel, "Sit at My Right Hand," 192–94.

God's.[56] For in an ultimate sense God *alone* is king (compare Sibylline Oracles 3.11; 1 Enoch 9.4; Philo, *On the Special Laws* 1, 30; *On the Virtues* 179; 1 Tim 6:15).[57] Understood in this historical context, then, the lordship of Psalm 110's Messiah is an exalted one indeed. And it is *this* understanding of the Messiah's lordly status that poses a problem for an exclusively Davidic understanding of his descent. How is *he*—this lordly co-regent of God's singular divine kingship—merely David's son?

This leads us to a second aspect of the inference that Jesus draws from Psalm 110:1. In Jesus' question in verse 37, αὐτοῦ is fronted (πόθεν αὐτοῦ ἐστιν υἱός), indicating emphasis: "how is he *his* son?" The point is not to deny the Messiah's sonship, but to deny that a merely Davidic ancestry could account for the Messiah's sovereign supremacy. The line of reasoning behind Jesus' question seems to be this: Given the Messiah's status as God's lordly co-regent, how can he merely be *David's* son? Matthew draws out the logic of Mark's question more straightforwardly: "*Whose* son is he?" (22:42). According to Jesus' riddle in Mark 12:35–37, the Messiah's lordly session in Psalm 110:1 requires us to conclude that he is ultimately "the son of someone other than David."[58]

Though Jesus' riddle only implies an answer to the question concerning the Messiah's sonship, the truth regarding his filial descent is not a mystery for the attentive reader of Mark.[59] At the beginning, middle, and end of his Gospel, Mark identifies Jesus the

---

56. Hengel, "Sit at My Right Hand," 156–57; Marcus, *Way*, 134; Bauckham, "Throne of God," 52–53.

57. Paul Rainbow identifies the ascription of exclusive sovereignty to God as one of "ten forms of explicit monotheistic speech" in Jewish Second Temple literature ("Monotheism and Christology in 1 Corinthians 8:4–6" [DPhil thesis, Oxford University, 1987], 45–46).

58. Marcus, *Way*, 141.

59. Ernest Best, *The Temptation and the Passion: The Markan Soteriology*, 2nd ed. (Cambridge: Cambridge University Press, 2005), 168.

Messiah as *the Son of God* (1:1, 11; 9:7; 15:39).[60] The structural location of these identifications within Mark's narrative lends support to Jack Dean Kingsbury's argument that the primary secret that Mark seeks to disclose to his readers is not so much the so-called *messianic* secret as it is the secret concerning Jesus' "divine sonship."[61] This is the secret that God and Jesus know (1:11; 9:7), and that the unclean spirits know as well (3:11; 5:7). It is moreover the secret that, for Mark, cannot be revealed fully within the context of Jesus' temple teaching, but only as he breathes his last on the cross (15:39).[62] It is in his lordly self-offering as a ransom for many (compare 10:45), wherein he fulfills the role scripturally patterned in the binding of Isaac,[63] that the Messiah's divine sonship is fully and finally unveiled: "Truly this was the Son of God!" (15:39).

For Mark, the secret of Jesus' status as God's lordly Son is intimated in the Old Testament Scriptures as well. Though the secret is *hidden* there, it is *there* (Rom 16:25–26). This is why Mark quotes Psalm 110, for verse 1 exhibits the lordly nature of God's anointed king. A question worth asking is whether the evangelist sees Psalm 110, taken as a whole, as the answer to Jesus' riddle. In verse 3 of the Septuagint, God speaks of the Messiah's eternal generation: "From the womb, before the morning star, I have begotten you."[64] Is this perhaps Mark's ultimate answer to Jesus' question regarding David's son? It is difficult to decide. A number of patristic interpreters certainly took it as such and concluded that God had

60. Joachim Gnilka, *Das Evangelium nach Markus* (Zürich/Neukirchen-Vluyn: Benziger/Neukirchener, 1979), 2:171.

61. Jack Dean Kingsbury, *The Christology of Mark's Gospel* (Philadelphia: Fortress, 1983), 14.

62. Compare Gnilka, *Markus*, 2:172.

63. See Best, *The Temptation and the Passion*, 167–72. For other associations of the Akedah with divine sonship, see Testament of Levi 18.6–7; John 3:16; Rom 8:32.

64. Psalm 110:3 in the MT is difficult to translate. Though it does not as clearly suggest the idea of eternal generation, Collins and Collins conclude that it does refer "to the begetting of the king" (Adela Yarbro Collins and John J. Collins, *King and Messiah as Son of God: Divine, Human, and Angelic Messianic Figures in Biblical and Related Literature* [Grand Rapids: Eerdmans, 2008], 19).

revealed his eternally begotten Son, even before the incarnation, to those like David who were his "friends and favorites."[65]

In response to Jesus' teaching, Mark tells us "the great crowd heard him gladly" (12:37). Once again, the contrast between the teaching of Jesus and that of the scribes is evident in the reaction of the crowd (compare 1:22).

EXEGETICAL AND THEOLOGICAL SYNTHESIS

One question remains for those who would follow the implications of this text to the point of theological understanding and confession: What does it mean within a Markan context to assert that Jesus is God's lordly Son? The answer to this question comes to light when we consider our passage in relation to both its immediate and broader contexts.

Jesus' parable in Mark 12:1–12 distinguishes his identity as God's "beloved son" from that of God's "servants" (especially 12:2–6). Not only does the beloved son come last in the series of emissaries (12:6), but he also stands in a relationship to the vineyard that is different from those who precede him. With his father, he owns the vineyard. He is "the heir" of its fruits (12:7). The distinction between the owner's beloved son and his servants is telling. And when this distinction is juxtaposed with Mark's monotheistic emphasis in 12:13–34, its significance becomes clear: Whereas it belongs to servants to gather the fruits that are due to *another*, it belongs to a beloved son to gather the fruits that are *his own*. The beloved Son alone is worthy, with his Father, to receive the fruits that are due him (compare 12:32). Consequently, the failure to respect the beloved Son (12:6) is tantamount to the failure to "render to God the things that are God's" (12:17).

---

65. John Chrysostom, *Homilies on the Gospel according to St. John*, Homily 8. Commenting on John 1:9, Chrysostom cites Mark 12:36 as evidence for David's vision of the preincarnate Son.

The characterization of Jesus' divine Sonship within the immediate context of 12:35–37 corresponds to what we find within the broader context of Mark's Gospel as well. In Mark's prologue, we learn that the "way" of the One sent by God to inaugurate the kingdom is "the way of the Lord" himself (1:2–3). Accordingly, as Mark's story unfolds, God's beloved Son appears as one who exercises the Lord's unique and incommunicable authority: forgiving sin (2:7, 10), perfecting the Sabbath (2:28), quieting the storm (4:41), walking on the sea (6:45–52), and so forth. The messianic Son who "comes *in the name of* the Lord" (11:9) comes *as* the Lord.[66] Moreover, the consummation of his coming is realized when, having given his life as a ransom for many, God's beloved Son sits enthroned as Lord at his Father's right hand (compare 12:10–11, 35–37; 14:62).

According to Mark's characterization, therefore, Jesus' identity as God's lordly Son signifies his status as one who, with God his Father, is the one true and living God. While this lordly characterization provides new meaning to the title "Son of God," which in the Old Testament can be accommodated to the title "son of David" (compare 2 Sam 7:12, 14), it provides this new meaning in a way that does not compromise biblical monotheism.[67] Mark does not wish to say that the Son is *another* god alongside God the Father (perhaps in the manner of an apotheosized emperor), but that he is one God *with* his Father. Just as Mark 12:35–37 presents two regents who share one divine throne, so Mark's Gospel as a whole presents two dramatis personae who share one divine life,

---

66. Rikk Watts offered a very similar reading of Mark's Gospel to that summarized in this and the two preceding sentences in a paper delivered at the Annual Meeting of the Society of Biblical Literature in November 2009 ("In the Power and Authority of God: A Preliminary Exploration of Yahweh Christology in Mark"). For another similar reading, see Bauckham, *Jesus and the God of Israel*, chapter 8.

67. Contra Wilhelm Bousset, *Kyrios Christos*, trans. John E. Steely (Nashville: Abingdon, 1970), 146–47.

power, and glory.[68] In doing so, Mark's Gospel exhibits the same Trinitarian grammar that is enshrined in the Nicene *homoousion*.[69] The Markan Son of God is "one of the Trinity."[70] Herein lies the glory of his identity; and herein lies the gravity of the decision with which those who meet him are confronted: Will they respect and receive him, and thereby enter into his kingdom and blessing, or will they disregard and reject him, and hence be trampled under his feet (compare Mark 12:36)?

The present interpretation further illumines the function of Mark 12:35–37 within the Markan plotline as a whole. Jesus' question regarding the Messiah's pedigree comes at the conclusion of his last public confrontation with the Jewish authorities on the stage of Mark's Gospel.[71] The next time Jesus faces this group is at his arrest and trial. There his accusers bring a number of charges against him that do not stick (14:55–59), until at last the charge of "blasphemy" prevails (14:60–64). At a minimum, the charge of blasphemy implies that Jesus had assumed certain unique divine prerogatives.[72] This charge is linked with Jesus' acceptance of the title "Son of the Blessed [One]," as well as his prediction of the Son of Man's enthronement "at the right hand of Power" (14:61–62),

---

68. C. Kavin Rowe speaks of a *Verbindungsidentität* of Jesus and God in Luke's characterization of Jesus (*Early Narrative Christology: The Lord in the Gospel of Luke* [Berlin: de Gruyter, 2006], 27). This notion applies to Mark's characterization as well.

69. Compare David S. Yeago, "The New Testament and the Nicene Dogma: A Contribution to the Recovery of Theological Exegesis," *Pro Ecclesia* 3 (1994): 152–64.

70. While Mark has relatively little to say about a third character who shares the singular life of God, it is instructive to note what he does say. According to Mark 12:36, it is "in the Holy Spirit" that David perceives and confesses the lordly nature of God's beloved Son (compare 1 Cor 12:3). The same Spirit who descends with God's fatherly approbation on Jesus at his baptism (1:10), and who overshadows him on the Mount of Transfiguration (9:7), is the One who unveils the glory of God's lordly Son to and through David. Given that only God can unveil God (compare 1 Cor 2:10-13), Mark's portrait of the Spirit confirms his identity as "one of the Trinity" as well.

71. Compare Mark 12:43, where Jesus calls his disciples to himself for private instruction. Jesus is not occupied with the Jewish leaders between 12:41 and 14:42.

72. Adela Yarbro Collins, "The Charge of Blasphemy in Mark 14:64," *JSNT* 26 (2004): 379–401.

two themes that also appear in 12:35–37. The question is: Whence did Jesus' accusers get the idea that his self-identification as the Son of God entailed a claim to unique divine prerogatives, thus opening him to the charge of blasphemy? In terms of the Markan narrative, it seems that Jesus' accusers derived this entailment from Jesus' own question in Mark 12:35–37. By proposing the idea of a lordly Son of God who shares God's singular sovereignty, Jesus introduced his opponents to a new understanding of messianic sonship and thus provided them with the very rope that they would use to hang him. Of course, it is a matter of no little dramatic irony that in providing his accusers with the grounds for his execution, Jesus also set the stage for the completion of his mission (compare 10:45) and the climactic unveiling of his identity as the Son of God on the cross (15:39). Mark 12:35–37 thus proves to be quite pivotal in Mark's characterization of Jesus as God's lordly Son.

HEIRS THROUGH GOD

GALATIANS 4:4–7 AND THE DOCTRINE OF THE TRINITY

Theological interpretation of Scripture is a human intellectual activity directed by and to the knowledge of the Triune God. In contemplating the special object of its attention, theological interpretation gives special consideration to the biblical *sedes doctrinae* (seats of doctrine) from which the doctrine of the Trinity emerges. To focus our interpretive energies on these particular texts is not to ignore the fact that the doctrine of the Trinity emerges most fully from "the antecedent logic of the Christian canon as a whole."[1] Nor is it to set aside the historical and literary forms of the texts under consideration.[2] The contemplation of *sedes doctrinae* is not a flight from historical-literary particularity but to historical-literary particularity insofar as such contemplation directs our thinking about particular doctrinal topics to the particular historical-literary "places"[3] where the prophets and apostles focus their attention on those topics.

---

1. C. Kavin Rowe, "The Trinity in the Letters of St Paul and Hebrews," in *The Oxford Handbook of the Trinity*, ed. Gilles Emery and Matthew Levering (Oxford: Oxford University Press, 2011), 42. More fully on this point, see Rowe, "Biblical Pressure and Trinitarian Hermeneutics," *Pro Ecclesia* 11 (2002): 295–312.

2. Compare the worries of Rowe, "Letters of St Paul," 43.

3. Consider the double meaning of *locus* in classical Protestant divinity.

Because the mystery of the Trinity has been revealed in the Scriptures under a form suitable to Adam's race, theology is drawn to the concrete "situatedness" that characterizes the apostolic embassy. In his letter to the Galatians, the apostle Paul does not speak in the tongue of angels; he speaks in Greek—and in one case, Aramaic. This historical-literary form of the apostolic communiqué is not obstacle to but occasion for the Spirit's illuminating presence: *through* Paul's epistolary representation of Christ crucified, the Spirit awakens in human hearts the Son's own filial cry, "Abba! Father!" (Gal 4:6; compare 3:1–5). Attention to the biblical *sedes doctrinae* thus enables theology to remain "within the verbal atmosphere of the text,"[4] which is the atmosphere within which theology lives and moves and has its being.

The purpose of the present essay is to contemplate the doctrine of the Trinity by considering one of its most venerable seats of doctrine, Galatians 4:4–7. How shall we proceed? Eduard Schweizer concludes his masterful study of New Testament filial sending language with the assertion that a Trinitarian theology is "already implied in the expression 'God sent his son.' "[5] Following on Schweizer's observation, the major focus in what follows will be on the question of how Galatians 4:4–7 implies a Trinitarian theology. Through an analysis of the grammar of divine agency exhibited in this text, I will argue that Paul construes God's act of realizing his son-making purpose through the missions of the Son and the Spirit as an act of God's immediate, natural agency. For Paul, to say that God acts through the Son and the Spirit is equivalent to saying that God acts "through God" (Gal 4:7), and therefore that the distinction between God, his Son, and the Spirit

---

4. R. R. Reno, "Biblical Theology and Exegesis," in *Out of Egypt: Biblical Theology and Biblical Interpretation*, ed. Craig Bartholomew, Mary Healy, Karl Möller, and Robin Parry (Grand Rapids: Zondervan), 396.

5. Eduard Schweizer, "What Do We Really Mean When We Say: 'God Sent His Son ...'?," in *Faith and History: Essays in Honor of Paul W. Meyer*, ed. John T. Carroll, Charles H. Cosgrove, and E. Elizabeth Johnson (Atlanta: Scholars Press, 1990), 312.

of his Son is not a distinction *between* God and other (perhaps creaturely? angelic? semi-divine?) agents but rather a distinction *within* God's own natural agency. Having discussed how Galatians 4:4–7 implies a Trinitarian theology, the concluding section of the essay will discuss briefly the sort of Trinitarian theology that our text implies, suggesting three elements that belong to a Trinitarian theology of Galatians.

THE TRINITY IN GALATIANS 4:4–7: HOW IS IT THERE?

The question of how Galatians 4 might imply a Trinitarian theology is caught up with the question of whether Galatians 4 presupposes the Son's preexistence. Based on his analysis of early Jewish and Christian examples of divine sending language, James D. G. Dunn argues that our text does not presuppose the Son's preexistence.[6] Others, such as Richard Hays and Gordon Fee, argue that it does.[7] While I would not go as far as F. F. Bruce and claim that the question of preexistence is "irrelevant" to Paul's argument here,[8] I do not think that our text speaks to the issue of preexistence with the same directness of other Pauline texts (for example, 1 Cor 8:6; 2 Cor 8:9; Phil 2:6–7). Nor do I think that preexistence is the most pertinent issue to consider when reflecting on our text's Trinitarian implications. I want to propose instead a different entryway into the Trinitarian claim of Galatians 4:4–7, specifically, by reflecting on the grammar of divine agency exhibited therein. If, as Wittgenstein suggests, grammar tells us what kind of object a thing is, then the question before us is this: *What kind*

---

6. James D. G. Dunn, *Christology in the Making: A New Testament Inquiry into the Origins of the Doctrine of the Incarnation*, 2nd ed. (Grand Rapids: Eerdmans, 1996), 38–44.

7. Richard B. Hays, *The Faith of Jesus Christ: The Narrative Substructure of Galatians 3:1–4:11*, 2nd ed. (Grand Rapids: Eerdmans, 2002), 96–111; Gordon D. Fee, *Pauline Christology: An Exegetical-Theological Study* (Peabody, MA: Hendrickson, 2007), 211–20.

8. F. F. Bruce, *The Epistle to the Galatians: A Commentary on the Greek Text*, NIGTC (Grand Rapids: Eerdmans, 1982), 195.

of action is the act whereby God sends his Son and Spirit in order to realize his son-making purpose for Israel and the nations? It is in discerning Paul's answer to this question, I contend, that we may best appreciate the Trinitarian claim implied in this text.

THE TWOFOLD MISSION OF THE SON AND THE SPIRIT AS AN INSTANCE OF IMMEDIATE DIVINE AGENCY

In Galatians 4:4–7, Paul describes the events whereby God's son Israel has been brought from a state of minority to a state of majority, and whereby Gentile Christians, formerly enslaved to τὰ στοιχεῖα τοῦ κόσμου (4:3, 9), have been brought to share in Israel's filial status and privilege. According to Paul, these events have come to pass through the twofold mission of the Son and the Spirit, which, as the summary of his argument in verse 7 makes clear, is equivalent to saying that these events have come to pass διὰ θεου (through God). What is the significance of describing events that occur through the Son and the Spirit as events that occur διὰ θεου? In describing the twofold mission of the Son and the Spirit in this way, Paul characterizes it as an instance of God's immediate action.

The contrast between God's immediate action (that is, that which God accomplishes by his own direct agency) and God's mediate action (that is, that which God accomplishes by the agency of another) runs throughout the Letter to the Galatians, representing one of Paul's "apocalyptic antinomies."[9] This contrast is what qualifies Paul's apostleship, which is "not from men nor through man but through Jesus Christ and God the Father" (οὐκ ἀπ' ἀνθρώπων οὐδὲ δι' ἀνθρώπου ἀλλὰ διὰ Ἰησοῦ Χριστοῦ καὶ θεοῦ πατρὸς) (1:1; see also 1:12). This contrast also seems to be

9. J. Louis Martyn, *Galatians: A New Translation with Introduction and Commentary*, AB 33a (New Haven: Yale University Press, 2004), 94.

one of the things that disqualifies the Mosaic law from being the means of realizing God's promise to Abraham. Whereas God is one, the Mosaic law is mediatorial in nature, delivered "through angels by the hand of a mediator" (δι' ἀγγέλων ἐν χειρὶ μεσίτου) (3:19–20), and this mediatorial nature of the law (somehow) contradicts the unilateral nature of the divine action required to accomplish Israel's promised eschatological deliverance.[10] The unspoken premise in Paul's argument seems to be drawn from Israel's prophets: as the deliverance of the first exodus was accomplished "not by elder or by angel but by the Lord himself" (Isa 63:9 LXX),[11] so too the deliverance of the second exodus must be accomplished not "by bow or by sword or by war or by horses or by horsemen" but "by the Lord their God" (Hos 1:7).

The aforementioned contrast between immediate and mediate divine agency is inscribed in the widely cited monotheistic formula, "not by means of an angel, not by means of a messenger." As Terrance Callan observes, this formula seems to emphasize the superiority of direct, unmediated divine action over indirect, mediated divine action.[12] The formula in turn expresses a common monotheistic conviction that "God's redemptive activity is always direct and unilateral in nature, reflecting the oneness of his person."[13] In terms of the text before us: Paul's claim that God has acted redemptively "through God" reflects this monotheistic

---

10. See further Richard N. Longenecker, *Galatians*, WBC 41 (Dallas: Word, 1990), especially 142–43; and Alan F. Segal, "'Two Powers in Heaven' and Early Christian Trinitarian Thinking," in *The Trinity: An Interdisciplinary Symposium on the Trinity*, ed. Stephen T. Davis, Daniel Kendall, and Gerald O'Collins (Oxford: Oxford University Press, 1999), 83.

11. For the relevance of Isaiah 63–64 to Galatians 4, see Rodrigo J. Morales, *The Spirit and the Restoration of Israel: New Exodus and New Creation Motifs in Galatians*, WUNT 2/282 (Tübingen: Mohr Siebeck, 2010), 26–28, 114–31.

12. Terrance Callan, "Pauline Midrash: The Exegetical Background of Gal 3:19b," *JBL* 99 (1980): especially 555–59. See also Longenecker, *Galatians*, 139-43.

13. Longenecker, *Galatians*, 143. Similarly Hans Dieter Betz, *Galatians: A Commentary on Paul's Letter to the Churches in Galatia*, Hermeneia (Philadelphia: Fortress, 1979), 172–73.

conviction regarding the superiority of immediate divine agency. What the law could not do—namely, bring to pass the redemptive realization of God's son-making purpose—God *himself* did through the missions of his Son and Spirit (compare Rom 8:3).

The immediate implication of this reading is obvious. By categorizing God's action through the Son and the Spirit as an instance of God's immediate saving action, Paul rules out the possibility of understanding the missions of the Son and the Spirit according to the pattern of creaturely emissaries, be they angels sent from heaven or prophets set apart from their mothers' wombs (compare Gal 1:15). The distinction between God, his Son, and the Spirit of his Son in carrying out God's redemptive purpose is not a distinction between God and other creaturely agents. It is rather a distinction within God's monotheistic agency.[14] In other words, God's singular saving agency is intrinsically threefold. We will return to this observation in due course.

THE TWOFOLD MISSION OF THE SON AND THE SPIRIT AS AN INSTANCE OF NATURAL DIVINE AGENCY

Categorizing God's redemptive action through the Son and the Spirit as an instance of God's immediate action does not exhaust the Pauline grammar of divine agency exhibited in this text. In order to more fully appreciate the character of divine action in Galatians 4:4–7, we must analyze the more specifically metaphysical dimensions of the Pauline grammar.

Metaphysical analysis of New Testament witness to the Trinity is repugnant to many modern biblical scholars, even to some who are otherwise sympathetic to Trinitarian readings of the biblical text. This attitude is commonly reflected in contrastive ways of summarizing biblical Trinitarianism. For example, Schweizer

---

14. For a discussion of Jewish antecedents, see Schweizer, "What Do We Really Mean," 300–301.

asserts that the language of divine sending in the New Testament "describes God in the category of his acts (dynamically) and not in that of his 'divine nature' (substantially)."[15] Although such assertions are not uncommon in contemporary theology,[16] I believe that they are misleading, and that they unnecessarily hinder a historical understanding of Paul's theology of divine agency.

Returning to the broader argument of Galatians 3:1–4:7 will help us appreciate the point. As we saw above, one of the things that disqualifies the law of Moses from being the means of fulfilling God's promises to Abraham is its mediatorial nature. The law's mediatorial nature somehow stands in contrast to the fact that God is one (3:19–20). Conversely, the immediate nature of God's redemptive action through the Son and the Spirit corresponds to the oneness of God's identity. The correspondence between God's identity and God's action provides a window into the frequently neglected metaphysical dimension of Paul's theology of divine agency.

Consider the correspondence between God's monotheistic being and God's monotheistic action in Galatians. As Hans Dieter Betz observes, "Paul's ... soteriology conforms throughout to the principle of oneness." God's singular *identity* is reflected in God's singular *acts*, and also in the singular creaturely *effects* of those acts. Again following Betz, for Paul there is one God (3:20), one messianic offspring (3:16), one gospel (1:6–7), one messianic people of God (3:28), and one fruit of the Spirit (5:22).[17] To this list we might add that, for Paul, there is one common object of ecclesial petition, though this common object is addressed, quite

15. Schweizer, "What Do We Really Mean," 309.

16. For two recent examples, see A. Edward Siecienski, *The Filioque: History of a Doctrinal Controversy*, Oxford Studies in Historical Theology (Oxford: Oxford University Press, 2010), 29; and Beverly Roberts Gaventa "Pentecost and Trinity," *Interpretation* 66 (2012): 12, 14.

17. Betz, *Galatians*, 173.

remarkably, in different languages: αββα, ὁ πατήρ (Gal 4:6; compare Rom 15:6).

These are not the only correspondences worth noting. Just as God's monotheistic saving action *includes* a distinction between God, his Son, and the Spirit of his Son, so too the creaturely effect of God's monotheistic saving action reflects a triadic structure: the one God is addressed as Father, in and with the Son, by the indwelling power of the Spirit (Gal 4:6).

What do these correspondences tell us about Paul's grammar of divine agency? Betz is probably right that these correspondences reflect the ancient rule, "like is the friend of like."[18] This rule is certainly reflected in other New Testament texts (for example, John 3:6; 1 Cor 2:12–15). I think, however, that more can be said in explanation of the correspondences between God's (Triune) identity, actions, and effects. One clue to the nature of these correspondences lies in the language Paul uses to describe God's agency in 4:7: διὰ θεου. Though perhaps not as pronounced as it is in other Pauline texts (for example, 1 Cor 8:6; Rom 11:36), Paul's use of the preposition "through" here likely signals his appropriation of ancient philosophical discourse related to "causality," discourse that other New Testament texts appropriate as well (John 1:1–3; Rom 11:36; 1 Cor 1:30; 8:6; Eph 4:6; Col 1:15–20; Heb 1:2; 2:10).[19] Paul and other New Testament authors draw on philosophical discourse of "prepositional metaphysics" to describe God's causal relation to the world.[20] In the language of Romans 11:36, God creates and providentially governs all things ("of him"), God is the providential end of all things ("to him"), and God himself providentially directs all things to their divinely appointed ends by means

18. Betz, *Galatians*, 173.

19. Robert M. Grant, "Causation and 'the Ancient World View,'" *JBL* 83 (1964): 34–40.

20. Gregory Sterling, "Prepositional Metaphysics in Jewish Wisdom Speculation and Early Christian Liturgical Texts," *The Studia Philonica Annual* 9 (1997): 219–38.

of his own wise agency ("through him").[21] In keeping with my earlier argument, I suggest that Paul employs the language of causality in Galatians 4:7 in order to express the monotheistic concern that God used no one else to carry out his work of eschatological redemption, but accomplished it by divine agency alone, solely by means of his Son and his Spirit. In other words, the metaphysical language of causality is well-suited to Paul's monotheistic concept of immediate divine agency.

Where does this get us? According to a widespread ancient conception of causality, certain *actions* and *effects* are exclusive to and indicative of certain *agents*. As noted above, for most Second Temple Jewish monotheists, the acts of creation and consummation belong exclusively to the agency of God: "They all were made through me alone, and through none other: by me also they shall be ended, and by none other" (4 Ezra 6:6). Some ancient thinkers explain the unique relation between an agent and his or her characteristic actions and effects with the concept of a natural (or proper) power. On this understanding, a natural power is one that is intrinsic to a specific kind of agent and therefore that, when exercised, signifies the agent by its effect. Thus, for example, Philo argues, "As it is the property of fire to burn, and of snow to chill, so also it is the property of God to be creating."[22] Some such conception of divine natural power arguably lies behind the correspondences between God's Triune identity, actions, and effects in Galatians 3:1–4:7. The Triune act of redemption to which Galatians 4:4–7 attests is not only an instance of God's *immediate* saving agency but also

---

21. Andrew Davison, *Participation in God: A Study in Christian Doctrine and Metaphysics* (Cambridge: Cambridge University Press, 2019).

22. Philo, *Allegorical Interpretation* 1.3 in *The Works of Philo Judaeus*, trans. C. D. Yonge (London: George Bell & Sons, 1800), 1:53. See further Michel René Barnes, *The Power of God: Δύναμις in Gregory of Nyssa's Trinitarian Theology* (Washington, DC: Catholic University of America Press, 2001).

an exhibition of God's *natural* saving power. "Salvation belongs to the Lord" (Ps 3:8).

This interpretation is confirmed when we turn from Galatians 4:4–7 to the exasperated question that immediately follows in verses 8–9. There the apostle asks, How can the Gentile Christians of Galatia, who have come to know the true and living God through the gospel, embrace the law of Moses, effectively turning back to the elementary principles of the cosmos? Paul's question presupposes the classical distinction between a true god, who is a god "by nature," and those that are falsely called gods "by human convention" (the λεγόμενοι θεοὶ of 1 Cor 8:5).[23] Much could be said regarding the significance of Paul's appeal to this distinction. For our present purposes, one observation is worth noting. In the present context, the mark that indicates the nondivine nature of the cosmic elements is their status as "weak and worthless." What is notable about this? I believe this represents one of the strongest arguments Paul can muster against his opponents in Galatia. Their teaching begets children for slavery; Paul's gospel begets children for freedom (see Gal 4:21–31). And this because his opponents' teaching yokes its recipients to those "that by nature are not gods" (4:8), and who therefore are naturally impotent to deliver from slavery, whereas the Pauline gospel flows from the One who is God by nature: the one true and living God who *is* Father, Son, and Spirit and who is therefore naturally potent to beget children of the living God (see Hos 1:10). Adoption and its attending filial cry, we might say, are natural signs of divine paternity, filiation,

---

23. Thus Augustine. See Eric Plumer, *Augustine's Commentary on Galatians: Introduction, Text, Translation, and Notes*, Oxford Early Christian Studies (Oxford: Oxford University Press, 2003), 183. More broadly on this distinction, see Walter Burkert, *Greek Religion*, trans. John Raffan (Cambridge, MA: Harvard University Press, 1985), chapter 7.

and spiration. To paraphrase Romans 8:3 again:[24] What the law could not do, weakened as it was by the flesh, God did, sending his own proper (ἰδίου) Son (Rom 8:32), and the Spirit of his Son, to redemptively beget children of God.

WHAT KIND OF TRINITARIAN THEOLOGY DOES GALATIANS 4:4–7 IMPLY?

In the foregoing analysis of Paul's grammar of divine agency, I have argued that Galatians 4:4–7 implies a Trinitarian theology insofar as it presents the twofold mission of the Son and the Spirit as an instance of God's immediate, natural agency. This is my answer, at least in part, to the question of how a doctrine of the Trinity is implied in this text. With this answer in place, I want to discuss briefly the question of what doctrine of the Trinity this text implies. I offer three summary points.

First, as we have seen, the distinction between God, his Son, and the Spirit in God's son-making activity is not a distinction between God and intermediary agents. It is rather a distinction within God's own immediate, natural agency. A Trinitarian theology of Galatians follows from reflecting closely on the *nature* of the distinction that is internal to God's monotheistic agency.

Second, Galatians 4:4–7 distinguishes the three agents internal to God's singular natural agency in two ways: by their named relations and by their various missions. In terms of the named relations: there is one who is named Father; there is one who is named his Son; and there is another who is named the Spirit of his Son. While these names are *intrinsic* to God's singular identity and action, they are also *irreducible* in relation to one

24. Romans 8:3 may be understood as an early Christian "commentary" on Galatians 4:4–7. See J. Louis Martyn, *Theological Issues in the Letters of Paul* (Edinburgh: T&T Clark, 1997), chapter 3.

another. The one name cannot be translated into another name. Indeed, each name entails an irreducible distinction from the others insofar as it signifies a "productive relation."[25] In the case of the present text: There is one who fathers and another who is fathered; there is one who breathes and another who is breathed.

In terms of their various missions: the three agents of God's singular agency are also distinguished insofar as there is one who sends (the Father) and there are two who are sent (the Son and the Spirit). Read within the context of the broader Pauline corpus, and the rest of the New Testament as well, we see that the various distinctions between sender and sendee correspond quite strictly to the named relations described above. The Father is sent by no one; but he sends forth his Son and the Spirit of his Son. The Son of the Father is sent by the Father; and he sends the Spirit. The Spirit of the Father and of the Son is sent by the Father and by the Son, though he himself sends no one. The "productive relations" that characterize the three in their irreducible distinctiveness are thus inflected in their missions.

Third, the gospel according to Galatians 4:4–7 is that the God who by nature is and acts as Father, Son, and Spirit acts not only in relation to himself but also in relation to us. If we are to grasp Paul's gospel of grace rightly, it is vital to observe the nature of God's Triune action in relation to us. Note well: While Paul's Trinity is unreservedly a Trinity for us, God's Triune action toward us is not what constitutes God as Trinity. The named relations of Father, Son, and Spirit are the presupposition of the missions, not their consequence. The named relations indicate the *agents* of God's monotheistic saving action, not its *effects*. Following a common apostolic pattern (see John 3:16–17; Rom 8:3, 32), Paul's letter to the Galatians complements the

---

25. As Thomas observes, "Divine Scripture uses, in relation to God, names which signify procession" (*Summa theologiae*, trans. Fathers of the English Dominican Province, 5 vols. [New York: Benziger Bros., 1948], I, q. 27, art. 1, resp.).

language of divine sending with the language of divine giving/self-giving: the sent Son is the one "who loved me and gave *himself* for me" (Gal 2:20). Rather than being acts of divine self-constitution, the missions are thus portrayed as acts of divine self-*giving* that graciously *extend* the Son's natural, internal relation to the Father *to us* (Gal 4:5: ἵνα τὴν υἱοθεσίαν ἀπολάβωμεν), with the result that (4:6: Ὅτι δέ ἐστε υἱοί) the Spirit of the Son cries out from within the hearts of Jesus' redeemed and adopted siblings, "Abba! Father!"

"By the work of adoption the likeness of natural sonship is communicated to men," Thomas Aquinas declares.[26] In so doing, God does not seek to supply his own wants but to communicate to us the abundance of his own intrinsic, natural, Trinitarian perfection.[27] This is the gospel of grace. This, ultimately, is what it means to be made "heirs through God."

26. Thomas Aquinas, *Summa theologiae*, III, q. 23, art. 1, ad 2; with Thomas Aquinas, *Commentary on Saint Paul's Epistle to the Galatians*, trans. Fabian Larcher (Albany: Magi Books, 1966), chapter 4, lecture 2.

27. Thomas Aquinas, *Summa theologiae*, III, q. 23, art. 1, ad 2; and art. 2, ad 3.

TO HIM WHO SITS ON THE THRONE AND TO THE LAMB

HYMNING GOD'S TRIUNE NAME IN REVELATION 4–5

The doctrine of the Trinity is central to the church's proclamation, prayer, and praise because it is central to scriptural teaching about God. If we care about retrieving Trinitarian teaching within the church, we must therefore also care about retrieving the doctrine of the Trinity's status as *scriptural* teaching. As David Yeago states, "No theory of the development of doctrine which attempts to save the classical doctrines without accounting for the unanimous conviction of the Christian tradition that they are the teaching of Scripture can overcome the marginalization of the doctrines which is so evident in the contemporary western church and theology."[1]

The relationship between holy Scripture and the church's doctrine of the holy Trinity is not self-evident. Some—content with the "assured results" of historical criticism or else absorbed with the narcissistic biblicism of certain forms of popular piety—don't even think to bring the Bible and the Trinity into the same conversation. While still others see a positive relationship between the Bible and the Trinity, they disagree about how to construe

1. David S. Yeago, "The New Testament and the Nicene Dogma: A Contribution to the Recovery of Theological Exegesis," *Pro Ecclesia* 3 (1994): 153.

the relationship. Some view the Bible as the yet unformed data of Trinitarian theology that later ecclesiastical reflection must process, clarify, and develop before we arrive at Trinitarian faith in the full-blooded sense. Others view the Bible as the expression of the early church's inchoate experience of the Trinity for which, once again, later ecclesiastical reflection must provide deeper ontological determination and sharper terminological clarification.

Both views, I believe, err in misconstruing the relationship between scriptural Trinitarianism and ecclesiastical Trinitarianism. Scriptural Trinitarianism is not unformed, inchoate Trinitarianism. As the self-revelation of the Triune God through his authorized and anointed prophets and apostles, scriptural Trinitarianism is the primary discourse of Trinitarian theology: normative, fluent, and eloquent. Ecclesiastical Trinitarianism, the Trinitarian theology of the church's sermons, hymns, confessions, and creeds, is the secondary discourse of Trinitarian theology. Ecclesiastical Trinitarianism, at its best, is the attempt to represent the "grammar" of Scripture's primary Trinitarian discourse in new settings and on new occasions, not to refine or develop what would otherwise be unrefined and undeveloped without it but to promote the church's greater fluency in reading Scripture's primary Trinitarian discourse and in responding to that discourse in its own eloquent expressions of prayer, proclamation, and praise of the Triune God.

I would like to focus on one particular scriptural text in considering the relationship between the Bible and the doctrine of the Trinity. That text is Revelation 4–5. Revelation 4–5 helps us gain greater fluency in Scripture's primary Trinitarian discourse in three specific ways.

First, Revelation 4–5 is one of Scripture's fullest presentations of Trinitarian theology. Revelation 4–5 presents all three persons of the Trinity. It presents the Trinity as the agent of creation, redemption, and consummation. And it presents well-ordered, indeed normative, worship of the Triune God.

Second, Revelation 4–5 presents its teaching on the Trinity in a manner with which we are less likely to be familiar. It does not use the standard terminology of "Father" and "Son" and "Holy Spirit" to identify the three persons of the Trinity. It does not say, "Jesus is Lord." Instead, it presents its teaching on the Trinity in the highly figurative language of apocalyptic literature: there is the throne, there is the Lamb, and there are the seven Spirits of God. But it is precisely this factor that makes Revelation 4–5 so instructive regarding the character of the Bible's primary Trinitarian discourse. Sometimes, we are lulled into thinking that we understand all too well what the Bible's Trinitarian language means. Revelation 4–5 does not allow this. It awakens us from the slumbers of our familiar miscomprehension of biblical language and forces us to pay attention more closely to the actual shape of the Bible's Trinitarian discourse. As we are drawn to contemplate more deeply the unfamiliar language and imagery of Revelation 4–5, we will discover its capacity "to evoke divine transcendence" and thereby to help us distinguish "true worship from idolatry, the true God from the false."[2]

Third, Revelation 4–5 presents what, from the vantage point of classical Reformed theology, is the consummate expression of human Trinitarian theology, the Trinitarian theology of the saints in heaven. In opening the door to God's heavenly court, Revelation 4–5 opens the door to the chorus of heavenly creatures and redeemed saints who have learned, in the Spirit and by virtue of the triumph of the Lamb, to praise with perfect eloquence the name of the holy Trinity. By showing us human theology in this consummate form, Revelation 4–5 thus sets the standard and goal

---

2. Richard Bauckham, *The Theology of the Book of Revelation*, New Testament Theology (New York: Cambridge University Press, 1993), 45–46.

for our Trinitarian theology as pilgrims who are still on the way to our everlasting rest: to gain, by the same Spirit, and by virtue of the same triumph of the Lamb, the fluency required to make us fitting participants in that heavenly chorus.

In looking at the presentation of the Trinity in Revelation 4–5, we will look primarily to the ways this text names the Trinity. The Triune God who presents himself to us in holy Scripture presents himself to us by means of divine names.[3] These divine names are the primary mode of divine self-revelation within Scripture's primary Trinitarian discourse. Consequently, as Basil affirms, when it comes to the manifold ways Scripture names God, "not one of the words that are applied to God in every use of speech should be left uninvestigated."[4]

My "investigation" will proceed in three steps. First, I will discuss briefly the grammar of divine naming, considering how God conveys his transcendent being, agency, and worth by means of ordinary patterns of creaturely naming. Second, I will discuss at greater length how Revelation 4–5 in particular names the Triune God, considering not only how each person is distinctly identified and glorified in these chapters, but also how they are related within God's undivided being, agency, and worship. Finally, I will conclude the discussion by considering, once again, the relationship between scriptural Trinitarianism and ecclesiastical Trinitarianism.

THE GRAMMAR OF DIVINE NAMING

In order to appreciate how Revelation 4–5 names the Trinity, we must consider for a moment the nature of naming more generally. This is not, as we will see, because divine naming is a species of

---

3. Scott R. Swain, "On Divine Naming," in *Aquinas Among the Protestants*, ed. Manfred Svensson and David VanDrunen (Hoboken, NJ: Wiley-Blackwell, 2018), 207–28.

4. Basil, *On the Holy Spirit*, trans. Stephen M. Hildebrand, Popular Patristics (Crestwood, NY: St. Vladimir's Seminary Press, 2011), 1.1.

naming in general. This is because God in his acts of naming himself for us in holy Scripture speaks to us in our language, making use of general patterns of naming to convey something of his transcendent being and glory.

THE GRAMMAR OF NAMING IN GENERAL

In considering the grammar of naming in general, we begin by distinguishing three paradigmatic acts of naming. (1) First, in naming we identify things—*this* tree, *this* cheeseburger, *this* human being. (2) Second, in naming, we *predicate* certain things of the things we identify—this tree is tall; this tree grew three feet over the past year. This cheeseburger is fresh; this cheeseburger became stale over the course of three hours. This human being is my husband. This human being was born on March 10, 1972. (3) Third, in naming, we *evaluate* the things we identify; we make judgments—this tree looks nice in our back yard; this tree is good for shade; this tree is good for climbing. This cheeseburger is the best cheeseburger I have ever eaten (a judgment we might make after eating at Culver's). This human being is reliable, honest, and bad at hanging towel rods.

These paradigmatic acts of naming, in turn, are performed in different ways. We may identify objects by means of definite descriptions, "the first man to walk on the moon"; by means of proper names, "Neil Armstrong"; and by means of various indicators, such as personal pronouns, "I," "you"; deictic terms, "this," "that," along with adverbs of place, adverbs of time, and tensed verbs.[5] Likewise, we *predicate* different sorts of things of objects by means of different kinds of predications. We predicate attributes—he is kind. We predicate actions—he bought me a cheeseburger. We predicate changes—his hair is growing gray (or

---

5. Paul Ricoeur, *Oneself as Another*, trans. Kathleen Blamey (Chicago: University of Chicago Press, 1995), 28–30. The specific examples are Ricoeur's.

falling out). And so forth. In similar fashion, we *evaluate* objects by means of various hierarchies of value.[6] When facing limited luggage space for travel, we must decide which is more important to us, our heavy coat or an extra pair of shoes. When determining which football teams will make it into the playoffs, we must weigh what matters more: number of wins, conference championships, strength of schedule, and so on. More significantly, when we distinguish objects across categories—say, distinguishing a "someone" from a "something"—we make different evaluations of an object's status, along with different determinations of the obligations we owe an object.[7] We may "use" a hammer, but a person we may not.

In each of these cases, acts of identification, predication, and evaluation involve judgments about an object's *relation to* and *distinction from* some larger category or family of which it is an instance or a member. As Robert Spaemann observes, "Nothing can be identified except *as a such-and-such*, which is to say, by virtue of a description that accommodates it alongside other things."[8] In identifying Neil Armstrong as "the first man to walk on the moon," we draw on a common class of beings ("man"), a common class of actions ("walk"), and a common class of settings in which such actions are capable of being performed (in this case, "moon"). But, in identifying Neil Armstrong as such-and-such an object who performed such-and-such an action in such-and-such a setting, we do so in order to set this particular object apart from other members of the common class.[9] We are not talking about men in general, walking in general, or planets in general. We are talking about *him*. He is "the first man to walk

---

6. Paul J. Griffiths, *Intellectual Appetite: A Theological Grammar* (Washington, DC: Catholic University of America Press, 2009), 24–28.

7. Robert Spaemann, *Persons: The Difference between "Someone" and "Something"* (New York: Oxford University Press, 2017), 5–15.

8. Spaemann, *Persons*, 124.

9. Ricoeur, *Oneself as Another*, 28.

on the moon." This identification is true of *this human being alone* and not of any other human being.

The same is true when it comes to acts of evaluation. When we call Neil Armstrong "the *first* man to walk on the moon," we are singling him out, acknowledging his pride of place within the pantheon of astronauts we have sent into outer space. But even then, we are singling him out as the first *in a series* of astronauts (and this is true even when the series of human beings to walk on the moon is only potential). The *best* football team in the country is still *one* football team among *many*. Evaluating the individual—whether it is a tree, a cheeseburger, or a human being—presupposes the existence of the larger class of which it or he is an instance or a member.

THE GRAMMAR OF DIVINE NAMING IN REVELATION 4–5

In John's vision, he sees and hears various things regarding the Triune God, which he reports to us by means of the ordinary grammar of naming. Revelation 4–5 *identifies* God by means of definite descriptions, as the "one seated on the throne" (Rev 4:2); by means of proper names and titles, as "the Lord God Almighty" (v. 8); and by means of indicators, as the one "who was and is and is to come" (v. 8). Moreover, Revelation 4–5 *predicates* certain actions of God. The heavenly host declares, "you created all things, and by your will they exist and were created" (4:8). Finally, Revelation 4–5 reports various acts of *evaluation* with reference to God: "Holy, holy, holy," the four living creatures proclaim day and night (4:8). And, because he is the supreme benefactor of all creaturely being and well-being, God is acknowledged as "Worthy … to receive glory and honor and power" (4:11).

While Revelation 4–5 draws on the ordinary grammar of naming to proclaim God's supreme excellence and worth, we should also observe that Revelation 4–5, following broader scriptural patterns, deploys that grammar in an extraordinary way. As we will see more fully below, when Revelation 4–5 identifies God, it does not identify him as a particular member of a larger class. When Revelation 4–5 predicates certain actions of God, it does not draw on a broader category of actions common to other agents. When Revelation 4–5 evaluates God's worth, it does not locate his worth on a larger scale of meaning and value. Revelation 4–5 takes up the ordinary grammar of naming to convey God's transcendent oneness, God's transcendent uniqueness in his being, action, and worth. The grammar of divine naming in Revelation 4–5 conveys that he alone is this one, that he alone does these things, that he alone is worthy of the worship he receives, that God is not in a class with creatures.

Revelation 4–5, moreover, engages in divine naming in a manner that is both triadic and doxological. All three persons of the Trinity are named in various ways in Revelation 4–5. There is the One who sits on the throne, there is the Lamb who stands in the midst of the throne, and there is the Spirit who is before the throne, who is identified as the Spirit of God and as the Spirit of the Lamb. Furthermore, John's vision of the holy Trinity comes by means of both sights and sounds that communicate divine glory. John sees God seated on a throne and apprehends his transcendent glory. John sees the Lamb standing as though it had been slain. And John sees a multitude of angelic hosts praising the Lamb. However, the primary mode of divine naming in Revelation 4–5 is not visual but aural. John hears one of the twenty-four elders proclaim the good news that the Lion of the tribe of Judah has overcome. And, more extensively, John hears the various hymns that various creatures in heaven, on earth, and in the sea raise to the Triune God in declaring his matchless worth. Among the variety of hymns John hears in Revelation 4–5 are the Trisagion, various acclamations of divine worth, a "new song" that celebrates the triumph of the Lamb, and a doxology.[10] In Revelation 4–5, divine hymning is the primary mode of divine naming.

The fundamental task of biblical interpretation in general and of Trinitarian theology in particular is thus to pay attention to the extraordinary ways in which Scripture deploys the ordinary grammar of naming to convey the transcendent being, activity, and worth of the Triune God. Doing so requires that we resist the temptation of allowing our preconceived notions about how things exist and act, and about how things should be regarded, to shape the way we interpret divine naming in holy Scripture. Rather, we must allow our minds, our judgments, and our speech to be trained and habituated in accordance with Scripture's unique way of revealing God's unique identity and worth.[11] Moreover, as Revelation 4–5 in particular emphasizes, because divine hymning is the ultimate form of divine naming that holy Scripture calls us to perform, being trained to follow scriptural patterns of divine naming ultimately involves being trained to follow scriptural patterns of divine praise. Only then can we begin to acknowledge the holy Trinity as he deserves to be acknowledged. Only then can we begin to worship the holy Trinity as he deserves to be worshiped.

PATTERNS OF TRINITARIAN NAMING IN REVELATION 4–5

In order that we may appreciate more fully how Revelation 4–5 conveys God's transcendent, Triune identity, activity, and worth by means of the ordinary grammar of naming, let us look at the specific ways it names the three persons of the Trinity. We will

10. Matthew E. Gordley, *New Testament Christological Hymns: Exploring Texts, Contexts, and Significance* (Downers Grove, IL: IVP Academic, 2018), 211.

11. Basil, *On the Holy Spirit* 4.6.

consider, first, the One who sits on the throne; second, the Lamb who stands in the midst of the throne; and third, the Spirit who is before the throne, the Spirit of God and of the Lamb.

THE ONE WHO SITS ON THE THRONE

John's heavenly vision of God in Revelation 4–5 may be described as a vision of "monarchical monotheism," a vision in which "God is seen as presiding over the heavenly court, in the celebration of the heavenly liturgy."[12] "At once," John says, "I was in the Spirit, and behold, a throne stood in heaven, with one seated on the throne" (Rev 4:2). John's description of the visible glory of the One seated on the throne is notably reticent in comparison to the visions on which he draws in Isaiah 6, Ezekiel 1, and Daniel 7 to articulate what he sees: "He who sat there had the appearance of jasper and carnelian" (v. 3). As Craig Koester notes, "John's reserve" in describing God's appearance "maintains a sense of God's transcendence so that he is not construed as a human being writ large."[13]

The One seated on the throne is encircled by three concentric circles "made up of first a rainbow, then a circle of the four cherubim," whose job it is to lead the heavenly liturgy, "then a circle of the twenty-four thrones upon which the twenty-four elders sit" (Rev 4:3, 5, 6–8).[14] From the throne "flashes of lightning," "rumblings and peals of thunder" come forth, redolent of the Lord's theophanic appearance at Mount Sinai (v. 5). Also before the throne are "seven torches of fire," which are identified as "the seven Spirits of God" (v. 5), and "a sea of glass, like crystal" (v. 6).

This initial way of "locating" God in Revelation 4-5 functions according to the grammar of divine naming described above.

---

12. John Behr, introduction to *Origen: On First Principles*, ed. and trans. John Behr (Oxford: Oxford University Press, 2018), xlv.

13. Craig Koester, *Revelation*, AYB 38a (New Haven: Yale University Press, 2015), 368.

14. David Aune, *Revelation 1–5*, WBC 52a (Dallas Word, 1997), 286.

While Revelation 4–5 employs the ordinary grammar of naming to identify God, locating him within the heavenly court, it does so in an extraordinary manner that precludes us from envisioning God as the member of a larger class of beings, or even as the biggest being around. As the one who is seated on his heavenly throne, he is portrayed as *supreme* above all creation.[15] As the one whose throne is encircled by a rainbow, the four living creatures, and the twenty four elders, he is portrayed as the *center* of all creation.[16] And, to recall an earlier identification of God in Revelation 1:8, as the one who is "the Alpha and Omega," he is portrayed as *the beginning and the end* of all creation. According to John's vision, the one who sits on the throne is not distinguished from creatures as the member of a broader class of creatures. John's vision names God as supremely transcendent and supremely unique. The One who sits on the throne is the transcendent Lord above all, the transcendent center of all, the transcendent beginning and end of all.

As John's vision proceeds from sight to sound, the various hymns of the four living creatures and the twenty-four elders further confirm the transcendent uniqueness of God. "Day and night," John tells us, the four living creatures "never cease to say, 'Holy, holy, holy, is the Lord God Almighty, who was and is and is to come' " (Rev 4:8). Here God is praised by his proper name and title, "the Lord God Almighty," a Greek way of representing the Hebrew proper name and title "YHWH of hosts." Unlike other names and titles that are commonly ascribed to both God and creatures in holy Scripture, this name and title is never ascribed to any creature. It is only ever ascribed to God alone. God is further

15. In Second Temple Judaism, the throne of God is one of the preeminent symbols of God's unique and unrivaled deity, signifying his status as the "*only* Sovereign" (1 Tim 6:15). See Richard Bauckham, "Throne of God and the Worship of Jesus," in *Jesus and the God of Israel: God Crucified and Other Studies on the New Testament's Christology of Divine Identity* (Milton Keynes, UK: Paternoster, 2008), 152–81.

16. Koester, *Revelation*, 382.

praised by means of an expanded version of his self-identification in Exodus 3:14. He is "the one who was and is and is to come," a name called on especially in circumstances where God's people suffer a mismatch between present realities and promised blessings, circumstances much like those of the seven churches Jesus has addressed in the preceding chapters. This manner of naming God indicates God's eternal and unchanging being, which is the grounds of God's faithfulness to his people and to his covenant promises throughout all the changes of history. Identifying God by his proper name and title and by his eternal and unchanging being, the heavenly creatures honor God as thrice-holy, an acclamation also reserved for God alone throughout Scripture, acknowledging that he is "set apart" from all creatures in his transcendent being, beauty, and worth.

According to John, the singing of the Trisagion by the four living creatures prompts the twenty-four elders to prostrate themselves before "him who is seated on the throne" and to worship "him who lives forever and ever" (Rev 4:9–10). Their worship consists in "a second-person acclamation of God's worthiness."[17] "Worthy are you, our Lord and God, to receive glory and honor and power, for you created all things, and by your will they exist and were created" (4:11). Speaking now not *of* him but *to* him, the heavenly creatures acknowledge God's absolute right to receive glory and honor and power. This right is rooted in his work of creation and providence.[18] As the sole benefactor of the world's coming to be and continuing to be, he alone is worthy of such praise. As all things are from him, so all praise is due him (1 Chr 29:10–19).

Once again, Revelation 4–5 employs the ordinary grammar of naming to extraordinary ends. The ordinary pattern of predicating and evaluating the action of a subject is here employed.

---

17. Gordley, *New Testament Christological Hymns*, 211.

18. Koester, *Revelation*, 365.

Subject A performed action X, and subject A's performance of action X makes him worthy of receiving honor Y. But, once again, the action predicated and the evaluation rendered are anything but ordinary. God is not identified as an ordinary agent who performs ordinary actions within the ordinary network of action and interaction that characterizes all creaturely action. God is identified as the intelligent cause of all creatures, of all creaturely action, and of the entire network of action and interaction within which creaturely action takes place: "by your will they existed and were created" (Rev 4:11). And this unique divine action of creation and providence, in turn, is the ground of his absolute regard. Worship, Revelation is keen to emphasize, is to be rendered to God alone because he alone is worthy. Though John is tempted on more than one occasion to worship one of the glorious heavenly envoys he runs into in the course of his vision, he is repeatedly rebuked and ordered to "worship God" (Rev 19:10; 22:9).

THE LAMB WHO STANDS IN THE MIDST OF THE THRONE

Revelation 5 begins with John's sight of a scroll in the right hand of him who is seated on the throne (Rev 5:1). This scroll, which is "written within and on the back" and "sealed with seven seals," in all likelihood represents God's hidden purpose for the world that he has made and that he providentially governs.[19] John then hears "a mighty angel" who asks "with a loud voice" the question, "Who is worthy to open the scroll and break its seals?" (v. 2). Who is able to understand God's sovereign purpose for creation? Who is able to bring God's sovereign purpose into effect?[20] The response causes John to "weep loudly" (v. 4). "No one in heaven

19. G. K. Beale, *The Book of Revelation: A Commentary on the Greek Text*, NIGTC (Grand Rapids: Eerdmans, 1999), 340–42.

20. Koester, *Revelation*, 384.

or on earth or under the earth was able to open the scroll or to look into it" (v. 3).

We should not pass too quickly by this response. Though we as readers know that the Lion and the Lamb will soon be identified as the One who is worthy to understand and effect God's sovereign purpose for creation, it is worth noting how he is identified even before he appears center stage in John's vision. He is *not* one of the things "in heaven or on earth or under the earth." Whoever it is who will be found worthy to open the scroll in God's right hand, he is not a creature. Before he is identified by his messianic names and titles, before majestic acts of deliverance are predicated of him, before he is acclaimed as worthy by all creatures in heaven and earth, he is distinguished from all creatures in heaven and earth. This one is not a member of that category. He too is identified by means of his transcendent oneness.

John then hears one of the twenty-four elders proclaim the good news: "Weep no more; behold, the Lion of the tribe of Judah, the Root of David, has conquered, so that he can open the scroll and its seven seals" (Rev 5:5). After hearing these glad tidings, John then sees "in the midst of the throne ... a Lamb standing, as though it had been slain, with seven horns and with seven eyes, which are the seven Spirits of God sent out into all the earth" (v. 6). In light of the previous determination in verse 5, this is quite an identification. The One who is not among the creatures that may be found in heaven, on earth, or under the earth is nevertheless identified by the most creaturely of creaturely descriptions, by a biographical description that is bracketed by "womb and tomb."[21] He is the Lion, born of the tribe of Judah. He is the Lamb who was slain.

It is precisely this pattern of christological naming that eventually led to the orthodox christological confessions of Nicaea and beyond. The One who is worthy to open the scroll and to effect

---

21. Robert W. Jenson, "For Us ... He Was Made Man," in *Nicene Christianity: The Future for a New Ecumenism*, ed. Christopher R. Seitz (Grand Rapids: Brazos, 2001), 75–86.

God's purpose for creation is on the divine side of the Creator-creature distinction. And yet this same One has the biography of a particular creature as well. Who can this be? How can this be? As Rowan Williams has recently argued, the church soon realized that both Judaism, with its array of heavenly angelic emissaries, and Greco-Roman culture, with its array of divinized human kings, lacked categories to account for the being and activity of the one identified in scriptural texts like Revelation 4–5. Attending to Scripture's unique patterns of christological naming eventually led the church to confess that this One is not a heavenly angelic emissary or a divinized human king but "one of the Trinity" who, for us and our salvation, came down from heaven, was born of the Virgin Mary, suffered under Pontius Pilate, was crucified, died, and was buried: Jesus Christ our Lord.[22]

After the Lamb had taken the scroll from God's right hand, the four living creatures and the twenty-four elders again fall down in worship, this time "before the Lamb" (Rev 5:8). In offering their worship, they hold not only harps but also "golden bowls full of incense, which are the prayers of the saints" (Rev 5:8). The Lamb, who has the seven horns, signifying divine power, and the seven eyes, signifying divine knowledge (Rev 5:6),[23] stands ready and able to receive the prayers of his suffering people, ready and able to respond to their pleas for deliverance.

And so the heavenly creatures sing a new song—again a "second-person acclamation,"[24] echoing themes from the first exodus—to celebrate the second exodus effected by the Lion and the Lamb in his death, resurrection, and ascension to God's right hand: "Worthy are you to take the scroll and to open its seals, for you were slain, and by your blood you ransomed people for God from every tribe and language and people and nation, and you have

---

22. Rowan Williams, *Christ the Heart of Creation* (London: Bloomsbury Continuum, 2018), 43–56.

23. Bauckham, *Theology of the Book of Revelation*, 112–13.

24. Gordley, *New Testament Christological Hymns*, 211.

made them a kingdom and priests to our God, and they shall reign on the earth" (Rev 5:9–10). Again note the sheer marvel of what is predicated of the One who stands in the midst of the throne. By means of the events of his very *human* biography, the Lamb has effected a uniquely *divine* act of redemption: ransoming God's people by his blood, making them a kingdom of priests to God. And because of his uniquely divine act of redemption, he is regarded by the heavenly chorus as worthy of the worship that is due to God alone.

John then sees and hears "the voice of many angels, numbering myriads of myriads and thousands of thousands," joining the heavenly chorus of the four living creatures and the twenty-four elders (Rev 5:11) and "saying with a loud voice, 'Worthy is the Lamb who was slain, to receive power and wealth and wisdom and might and honor and glory and blessing' " (5:12). As the One who sits on the throne has been acknowledged as worthy because of his work of creation and providence, receiving the threefold acclamation of "glory and honor and power" (4:11), now the Lamb who is in the midst of the throne is acknowledged as worthy because of his work of redemption to receive the sevenfold acclamation of "power and wealth and wisdom and might and honor and glory and blessing" (5:12).

Perhaps because the sevenfold praise of the Lamb corresponds to his work of completing or perfecting God's purpose for creation, the expanding chorus of praise then extends from heaven to include "every creature ... on earth and under the earth and in the sea, and all that is in them" (5:13). This time God and the Lamb are hymned together, and this time by means of a doxology:[25] "To him who sits on the throne and to the Lamb be blessing and honor and glory and might forever and ever" (v. 13). This doxology is met, in turn, with the "Amen!" of the four living

25. Gordley, *New Testament Christological Hymns*, 211.

creatures, which prompts the twenty-four elders, once again, to fall down and worship (v. 14).

To summarize, according to Revelation 5, the One who stands in the midst of the throne is not numbered among God's creatures in heaven or on earth or under the earth. He is identified by his transcendent oneness. Nevertheless, this transcendent one has a human biography, being born of the tribe of Judah, and having suffered a violent death. Moreover, by his means of the events of his human biography, this one has effected divine redemption on behalf of his people, ransoming them by his blood and making them a kingdom of priests to God, thereby completing and perfecting God's purpose for creation as he alone is qualified to do. For this reason, the One who stands in the midst of the throne receives glory and honor from all creatures, not as "a second object of worship alongside God," but as one who is "included in the worship due the one God."[26]

THE SPIRIT WHO IS BEFORE THE THRONE

The focus of divine naming and divine hymning in Revelation 4–5 falls on the first and second persons of the Trinity, on the One who sits on the throne and on the Lamb who stands in the midst of the throne. However, Revelation 4–5 is not silent when it comes to the third person of the Trinity, the Spirit who is before the throne. The ways these chapters name him therefore repays our careful attention as well.

The vision that Jesus shows John in Revelation 4–5 is a vision that John receives "in the Spirit" (4:2). This is in keeping with the broader pattern of divine communication on display across Revelation as a whole. God has given to Jesus a revelation to deliver to John (1:1). This revelation, in turn, is received by John and by the seven churches by means of the Spirit's agency. All that John sees and all that John hears regarding the One who sits

26. Koester, *Revelation*, 392.

on the throne and regarding the Lamb who stands in the midst of the throne, and all that John passes on to the seven churches, comes about "in the Spirit."

"The testimony of Jesus" is given by "the Spirit of prophecy." And the Spirit of prophecy is clear: "worship God" (Rev 19:10), which according to Revelation 4–5 means "worship God and the Lamb." But what about the Spirit? Where does Revelation locate him, how is he identified, what is predicated of him, and how is his person evaluated? Though some commentators identify "the seven Spirits of God" in Revelation 4:5 as angelic beings, closer analysis leads to the conclusion that this is a misidentification and a misevaluation.[27]

The Spirit's location "before the throne" (Rev 4:5) is admittedly an ambiguous identification. This location is also ascribed to creatures and the sea of glass (4:6), as well as those who appear in God's presence for judgment (20:12). However, among those who are located *before* the throne, he alone is described as belonging to the One who sits *on* the throne and to the One who stands *in the midst of* the throne (4:5; 5:6). "The seven Spirits of God" in Revelation 4:5, taken along with the seven horns and the seven eyes in Revelation 5:6, is undoubtedly a reference to Zechariah 4:1–14. In the latter text, "the seven eyes of the Lord" are identified by the Lord as "my Spirit."[28] The identity of the Spirit is therefore clear. The Spirit *before* the throne is the Spirit *of* the two who are *on* the throne. The Spirit *before* the throne is the Spirit who proceeds "*from* the throne of God and of the Lamb" (Rev 22:1).

By identifying the Spirit with the seven horns and the seven eyes possessed by the Lamb, John further identifies the Spirit with God's transcendent power and God's transcendent knowledge as one who is therefore able to bring God's creative and redemptive

---

27. Malcolm B. Yarnell III, *God the Trinity: Biblical Portraits* (Nashville: B&H Academic, 2016), 211–17.

28. Bauckham, *Theology of the Book of Revelation*, 110–11.

purpose, accomplished by Jesus, to its goal by empowering the prophecy, prayer, and praise of God's people in the midst of an idolatrous world.[29] In the Spirit, the redemptive purpose of God for creation, the purpose unveiled and enacted by the Son, is brought to completion.

This identification is confirmed when we look more broadly at John's letter as a whole. In the opening salutation, John does not offer the typical dyadic Christian greeting, wishing grace and peace to the seven churches from God the Father and from the Lord Jesus Christ. Instead he offers a unique triadic greeting: "Grace to you and peace from him who is and who was and who is to come, and from the seven Spirits who are before his throne, and from Jesus Christ" (Rev 1:4–5). In other words, John locates the Spirit, along with God and Jesus, on the divine side of the Creator-creature distinction, characterizing him as an agent of divine blessing.[30] Moreover, in Jesus' address to the seven churches, the churches are repeatedly urged to "hear what the Spirit says to the churches" (2:7, 11, 17, 29; 3:6, 13, 22). This is a noteworthy repetition. In enjoining the churches to listen to the Spirit of God, Revelation enjoins the churches to perform the first and fundamental act of worship they owe to the one true God: "*Hear*, O Israel ..." (Deut 6:4).

With the One who sits on the throne and with the Lamb who stands in the midst of the throne, John thus locates the Spirit, who is before the throne on the divine side of the distinction between Creator and creature, as the source of all divine blessing, as one who is worthy of all divine honor. According to the revelation given by Jesus to John, we honor the third person of the Trinity by heeding the Spirit of prophecy, who enjoins and empowers us to render "blessing and honor and glory and might forever and ever" "to him who sits on the throne and to the Lamb" (Rev 5:13).

---

29. Bauckham, *Theology of the Book of Revelation*, 112–15.

30. Bauckham, *Theology of the Book of Revelation*, 23–24.

THE INDIVISIBLE, INTERNALLY ORDERED BEING, AGENCY, AND WORSHIP OF THE TRINITY ACCORDING TO REVELATION 4–5

Though Revelation 4–5 names the One who sits on the throne, the Lamb who stands in the midst of the throne, and the Spirit who is before the throne in three distinct ways, it does so without compromising scriptural monotheism, without suggesting the existence of three gods. Revelation 4–5 characterizes the holy Trinity as indivisible and internally ordered in his being, agency, and worship. How so?

While Revelation 4–5 recognizes the presence of many thrones in heaven, the three persons of the Trinity share one throne. As we have seen, the throne of God symbolizes God's transcendent oneness, indicating his supremacy over all creatures, his centrality to all creatures, and his status as the beginning and end of all creatures. From this we may conclude that, although the three persons are distinguished by various means of identification and predication in Revelation 4–5, because they share one divine throne they share God's transcendent oneness. Moreover, the fact that both God and the Lamb share the seven Spirits of God also indicates their transcendent oneness.[31]

Although Revelation 4–5 appropriates the work of creation and providence to the One who sits on the throne, the work of redemption to the Lamb who stands in the midst of the throne, and the work of sanctification to the Spirit who is before the throne, the identification of the three persons with these three distinct moments of God's unfolding kingdom should not be taken to suggest that they act *serially* within that unfolding kingdom: first the Father, then the Son, and finally the Spirit. For one thing, Revelation elsewhere ascribes the works of creation and consummation to the second person of the Trinity (Rev 1:17; 3:14; 22:13).[32]

---

31. Koester, *Revelation*, 387.

32. Bauckham, *Theology of the Book of Revelation*, 54–58.

For another thing, Revelation elsewhere exhibits the Greek grammatical oddity of using a singular verb to describe the reign of God and of the Lamb, thus violating the basic rule of subject-verb agreement (Rev 11:15; 22:3).[33] From this we may conclude that the distinction between the first, second, and third persons of the Trinity in enacting the unfolding kingdom of God is not a distinction between three agencies. It is rather a distinction within one divine agency. The three persons who share one divine throne enact one divine agency.

Though Revelation 4–5 progresses from the worship of the One who sits on the throne to the worship of the Lamb who stands in the midst of the throne, these chapters conclude with the worship of the One who sits on the throne and of the Lamb. That this is the climactic expression of worship in Revelation 4–5 indicates that Revelation does not envision the worship of two or three gods. Instead it envisions the worship of one God in three persons. In the Spirit, Revelation calls us to worship God and the Lamb.

Though it does not receive the same degree of emphasis in these chapters as it does elsewhere in John's writings, Revelation 4–5 does indicate something about the character of the distinction that obtains among the three persons of the Trinity within the transcendent oneness of God's being and agency. According to these chapters, the revelation that John receives comes from God, by Jesus, in the Spirit. In similar fashion, God's hidden purpose for creation is accomplished by Jesus and applied by the Spirit, sent out into all the earth. Here, as we have already seen, we are not dealing with a distinction between three divine agencies. We are dealing with distinctions within one divine agency. What is the character of that distinction? According to Revelation 4–5, the singular agency of God proceeds from the One who sits on the

33. Bauckham, *Theology of the Book of Revelation*, 60–61.

throne, through the Lamb who stands in the midst of the throne, in the Spirit who is before the throne.

Is there anything more that can be said regarding the relation between the persons, not only within God's undivided agency, but also within God's undivided being? I believe there is. Though we have to look elsewhere in Revelation to find the distinction between the first and the second persons of the Trinity, described as the relation between the Father and the Son (for example, Rev 3:21), Revelation 4–5 identifies the Spirit in such a way that indicates something fascinating about his personal identity as the third person of the Trinity. Specifically, the Spirit is described, in rather symmetrical fashion, as belonging to both the One who sits on the throne and the One who stands in the midst of the throne. He is the Spirit of God and of the Lamb. While this is not exactly a full-blooded statement of the Spirit's eternal procession from the Father and the Son, it is a striking image of his relation to the Father and the Son nonetheless.

SEVEN AXIOMS

ON THE TRINITY, THE BIBLE, AND THEOLOGICAL INTERPRETATION

A long tradition of modern biblical criticism regarded the doctrine of the Trinity as a late development in the evolution of doctrine, traceable perhaps to terms and themes in the New Testament text but not itself contained and communicated therein. Theological interpretation of Scripture represents a conversion from this perspective. Theological interpretation of Scripture rests on the conviction that the Trinity precedes, not just biblical interpretation, but the Bible itself. The Bible and its interpretation are downstream, not upstream, from the Trinity, products of the Triune God's willingness to make himself the object of creaturely knowledge, love, and beatitude. The seven theses that follow, along with their brief explanation and expansion, summarize this conversion and offer a framework for thinking about the relationship between the Trinity, the Bible, and theological interpretation of Scripture:

1. Certain material and social conditions are vital to, but not ultimately sufficient for, theological interpretation of Scripture.
2. The Trinity's knowledge of the Trinity is the ontological foundation of our knowledge of the Trinity.
3. The Trinity reveals the Trinity by the Trinity; this is the epistemological foundation of our knowledge of the Trinity.
4. The Trinity reveals the Trinity by the Trinity in an economy that is first mediate, in the state of pilgrims, then immediate, in the state of the blessed.
5. The mediate revelation of the Trinity by the Trinity in the state of grace presupposes and illumines vestiges of the Trinity in the state of nature.
6. The mediate revelation of the Trinity by the Trinity in the state of grace comes in the twofold embassy of prophetic and apostolic revelation in Holy Scripture.
7. The immediate revelation of the Trinity by the Trinity in the state of glory is the supreme good and final end of theological interpretation of Scripture.

EXPLAINING THE AXIOMS

1. CERTAIN MATERIAL AND SOCIAL CONDITIONS ARE VITAL TO, BUT NOT ULTIMATELY SUFFICIENT FOR, THEOLOGICAL INTERPRETATION OF SCRIPTURE

In theological interpretation of Scripture, faith devotes loving attention to the historical and literary shape of scriptural texts that it might discern the singular being and activity of the Triune

God who presents himself therein as our Maker, Redeemer, and Reward. Theological interpretation of Scripture is faith-seeking, interpretive understanding, the intelligent and loving grasp of the Triune God, the supremely intelligible, supremely adorable good.

Success in this enterprise presupposes both material and social conditions. The material conditions of theological interpretation of Scripture afford the undistracted leisure that acts of interpretive attention require. Holy Scripture is written in such a way that the reader may run (Hab 2:2). But the reading of holy Scripture becomes most profitable when readers are afforded the space and time necessary to devote themselves to the patient, contemplative study, practice, and teaching of holy Scripture (Ezra 7:6, 10; Luke 10:39).

The material conditions of theological interpretation of Scripture, in turn, flourish in relation to certain social conditions, which provide the setting in which the gifts of interpretive understanding are received and shared. Theological interpretation of Scripture is no solo enterprise, either in origin or destination. The student of Scripture must first be taught if she is to succeed (2 Pet 3:16). And her success in scriptural interpretation requires that she share her gifts of interpretive understanding with others (Rom 12:6–7). The knowledge of the Triune God conveyed in holy Scripture is received "with all the saints" (Eph 3:18) for the building up of all the saints in the knowledge of the Triune God (Eph 4:12–13).

Though vital to the task of theological interpretation, the material and social conditions of faith's quest for interpretive understanding are not, in themselves, sufficient for this quest to flourish. The Triune God alone is sufficient for these things: from him and through him and to him faith's quest for theological understanding succeeds. The being and agency of the Triune God are the ultimate context within which theological interpretation of Scripture flourishes. In him, theological interpretation of Scripture lives and moves and has its being.

2. THE TRINITY'S KNOWLEDGE OF THE TRINITY IS THE ONTOLOGICAL FOUNDATION OF OUR KNOWLEDGE OF THE TRINITY[1]

Because God is light and nothing but light (1 John 1:5), the being of God is intelligible and adorable: pure truth, pure goodness, pure beauty. "How lovely is your dwelling place, O Lord of hosts!" (Ps 84:1). Because the being of God is intelligent and adorable, the life of God is a life of intelligence and adoration. God knows and loves himself. And God's beatitude or blessedness consists in God perceiving the truth of his being and delighting in its goodness. The "blessed and only Sovereign" "dwells in unapproachable light" (1 Tim 6:15, 16).

The being and life of the blessed God is only one (1 Tim 6:15). But as the being of the one God is tripersonal in its mode of being, so the life of the one God is tripersonal in its mode of knowledge, love, and beatitude. The Father knows and delights in the Son (Matt 11:27; Mark 1:11). The Son knows and rejoices in the Father (Matt 11:25, 27). The Spirit alights on the Father's beloved Son (Mark 1:11). In the Spirit, the Son rejoices in the Father (Luke 10:21). The blessed and only Sovereign is the blessed Trinity.

The knowledge, love, and beatitude of the blessed Trinity is unapproachably high and holy (1 Tim 6:16), hidden not because it is dark or arcane but because it is supremely luminous, supremely lovely—surpassing what human eyes can see or human hearts can imagine (Job 28; 1 Cor 2:9). "No one knows the Son except the Father, and no one knows the Father except the Son" (Matt 11:27). "No one comprehends the thoughts of God except the Spirit of God" (1 Cor 2:11). For this reason, only the blessed Trinity can make the blessed Trinity known (Matt 11:26–27; 1 Cor 2:10–12). Only

1. The architectonic framework that underlies axioms 2, 3, 4, and 7 is drawn from Franciscus Junius, A *Treatise on True Theology*, trans. David C. Noe (Grand Rapids: Reformation Heritage Books, 2014).

the blessed Trinity can make others blessed in the knowledge and love of the Triune God.

Thanks be to God, the Triune God, who is blessed in the knowledge and love of himself and who wills to make us blessed by making himself the object of creaturely knowledge and love. This is the Father's "good pleasure" (Matt 11:26), what the Son "chooses to reveal" (Matt 11:27), what the Spirit freely gives (1 Cor 2:10, 12; 12:11). The Triune God wills to grant us rest by causing us to know and love himself (Matt 11:28–30). Here is the ontological foundation of our knowledge of the Trinity: we may be blessed in the knowledge and love of the Trinity because the Trinity is blessed in the knowledge and love of himself and because he wills to make us blessed in the knowledge and love of himself.

3. THE TRINITY REVEALS THE TRINITY BY THE TRINITY; THIS IS THE EPISTEMOLOGICAL FOUNDATION OF OUR KNOWLEDGE OF THE TRINITY

Because the knowledge and love of the persons of the Trinity is high and holy (1 Tim 6:16), transcending all other possible objects of knowledge and love, the persons of the Trinity must stoop down to our level to make themselves known (Isa 57:15; John 1:18). Because the knowledge and love of the persons of the Trinity is internal to the Trinity (1 Cor 2:11), not evident on the surface of their indivisible works, the persons of the Trinity must open that knowledge and love to us if we are to receive it and enjoy it (1 Cor 2:12). The revelation of the Trinity is *self*-revelation in the strict sense. The persons of the Trinity alone reveal the persons of the Trinity. "No one knows the Father except the Son and anyone to whom the Son chooses to reveal him" (Matt 11:27). "No one comprehends the thoughts of God except the Spirit of God. Now we have received not the spirit of the world, but the Spirit who is from God, that we might understand the things freely given us by God" (1 Cor 2:11–12).

Not only do the persons of the Trinity reveal themselves, the persons of the Trinity reveal themselves by themselves. The Son comes in person to reveal the Father (John 1:18). The Spirit comes in person to give us the knowledge of the Father in the Son (Gal 4:6). The effects of the persons' comings raise questions about the persons' modes of being: "Who then is this?" (Mark 4:41). But only the persons themselves can answer those questions: "This is my beloved Son" (Mark 9:7). In similar fashion, the address of human ambassadors and emissaries is effectual as Trinitarian revelation only because the divine persons themselves present themselves to us through their human ambassadors and emissaries (2 Cor 5:20; 1 Thess 2:13). The Son himself reveals what the Spirit, by David, taught us that the Lord said to the Lord (Mark 12:35–36). The Spirit himself takes what the Father has given to the Son and reveals it to and through the apostles (John 15:26–27; 16:13–15).

The revelation of the Trinity is tripersonal discourse in a strong sense: the persons of the Trinity reveal the persons of the Trinity by the persons of the Trinity. The Trinity illumines the Trinity by the Trinity's own light; the Trinity satisfies our thirst for the Trinity by satiating us from the fullness of the Trinity's own fountain (Ps 36:9). The Triune God is his own interpreter.

4. THE TRINITY REVEALS THE TRINITY BY THE TRINITY IN AN ECONOMY THAT IS FIRST MEDIATE, IN THE STATE OF PILGRIMS, THEN IMMEDIATE, IN THE STATE OF THE BLESSED

The Triune God reveals himself now "in a mirror dimly," in the state of pilgrims, then "face to face," in the state of the blessed (1 Cor 13:12; Exod 33:20). God's revelation now is *self*-revelation, a revelation of the Trinity by the Trinity. But it is *mediated* self-revelation. The Trinity reveals himself by himself through created works and created words. The Word became flesh and dwelt among us and explained the Father to us in Aramaic and Greek (Mark 14:36; John 1:14, 18). The Triune God personally addresses us by means of the address of his prophets and apostles (2 Cor 5:20).

Our "blessed hope" is the "appearing" of Jesus Christ in visible glory (Titus 2:13). In and through Jesus Christ the Son of God, we will see the Father's face and drink of the Spirit without the veil of creaturely media. In the state of the blessed, the Triune God will enlighten us by his own unmediated light and will satisfy us by his own unmediated life (Rev 22:1–5). We will see the Triune God and be satisfied in the Triune God by the Triune God.

5. THE MEDIATE REVELATION OF THE TRINITY BY THE TRINITY IN THE STATE OF GRACE PRESUPPOSES AND ILLUMINES VESTIGES OF THE TRINITY IN THE STATE OF NATURE[2]

As God is our Maker, Redeemer, and Perfector, so he reveals himself in the threefold economy of the state of nature, the state of grace, and the state of glory. Though God reveals much about his eternal being and glory in the state of nature (Ps 19; Rom 1:19–20), he does not reveal his triunity, at least not directly. The tripersonal being of God is high and holy, an unapproachable light (1 Tim 6:16). The tripersonal being of God exceeds God's created effects, much in the way the inner life of an artist exceeds his artwork (1 Cor 2:11). Therefore, it is impossible to reason from God's created and providential effects to God's tripersonal life. The Trinity reveals the Trinity by the Trinity: now in a mirror

2. The present axiom is my attempt to do justice to a reality heretofore I have ignored, but which henceforth I may not due to Katherine Sonderegger, *Systematic Theology, Volume 2, The Doctrine of the Holy Trinity: Processions and Persons* (Minneapolis: Fortress, 2020), chapter 2.

dimly, in the state of grace, then face to face, in the state of glory (1 Cor 13:12).

The state of nature is not, for that reason, immaterial to the self-revelation of the Trinity in the state of grace. Though the Triune cause of all creatures exceeds its creaturely effects, its creaturely effects bear a distant resemblance or similitude to their Triune cause. This is especially true of human beings, creatures made in the image of the Triune God.

The distant resemblance or similitude of creatures to the Trinity means there is no one-to-one correspondence between creatures and the Trinity. All attempts at finding such a correspondence between, say, human fathers and human sons and the divine Father and the divine Son inevitably end in theological error. Human beings are made in the image of the Triune God (Gen 1:26). But the Triune God is not in a class with creatures, not even with human beings (Isa 40:18). Whatever similarities hold between the being of the creature and the being of the Trinity pale in comparison to their dissimilarities.

Nevertheless, due to the distant resemblance or similitude of creatures to the Trinity, the Triune God can speak in the language of the creature, whose native habitat is the being of the creature, in such a way that the language of the creature becomes a revelation of the Triune God. Scripture sees creaturely vestiges of the Trinity, neither in triadic patterns, nor in creation's unity and diversity, but in various relations between creatures and within creatures. God in Scripture takes up the relations between human fathers and human sons, of human persons to human speech, of the human spirit to human thoughts, of the sun to its rays, and of fountains to the rivers that flow therefrom, and deploys them, with new sense and significance, to reveal himself as the Father of a radiant Son, as the Spirit who searches the depths of God, and as the Source of a river of living water.

Creatures are mere vestiges of the Trinity. But they are truly vestiges, made and therefore fit to be taken up and redeployed by the Trinity in the revelation of the Trinity, causing God's Triune light to be seen by means of their vestigial lights.

6. THE MEDIATE REVELATION OF THE TRINITY BY THE TRINITY IN THE STATE OF GRACE COMES IN THE TWOFOLD EMBASSY OF PROPHETIC AND APOSTOLIC REVELATION IN HOLY SCRIPTURE

In the state of grace, wherein God brings human beings out of the state of estrangement and devastation brought upon them by Adam's sin and into the blessed state of covenant union and communion with God through the person and work of Jesus Christ, the Trinity reveals the Trinity by the Trinity through the embassy of prophets and apostles in holy Scripture. The revelation of the Trinity through the twofold embassy of prophets and apostles unfolds according to the logic of a divine mystery. The Trinity, once hidden in the Old Testament, is more fully revealed in the New Testament.[3]

The relationship between Old Testament and New Testament revelation of the Trinity is not the relationship between shadow and substance or between type and antitype. The Trinity's hiddenness in the Old Testament is not a mode of absence. Hiddenness is a mode of divine presence. The Trinity's hidden presence is manifest, among other ways, in triadic portraits of divine agency (for example, Gen 1; Ps 33:6) and in mysterious conversations between the Lord and other speech agents (for example, Pss 2; 45; 110; Prov 8). Old Testament revelation of

3. The amplest statement of the present point, made with admirable clarity, is Fred Sanders, *The Triune God* (Grand Rapids: Zondervan Academic, 2016).

the Trinity is, as B. B. Warfield said, a room "richly furnished but dimly lighted."[4]

In the incarnation of the Son and the outpouring of the Spirit, the persons of the Trinity are present among God's people in new ways, bringing a new and fuller revelation of the Trinity. The New Testament reveals the Trinity by attesting acts of divine self-naming (for example, Matt 11:25–27; Mark 1:11; 12:35–37; John 16:13–15), by announcing the missions of the Son and the Spirit (for example, Mark 12:1–12; Gal 4:4–7), and by hymning the Trinity's relation to the cosmos (for example, John 1:1–18; Col 1:15–18). These various modes of New Testament Trinitarian revelation often employ the language of the Old Testament, making clear what is there concealed. The New Testament also includes texts that exhibit highly synthesized and organized summaries of Trinitarian revelation (for example, Matt 28:19; 2 Cor 13:14; Eph 4:4–6; Rev 1:4–6). This scriptural pattern of teaching (Rom 6:17; 2 Tim 1:13) is foundational to later ecclesiastical summaries of Trinitarian teaching (for example, the rule of faith).

7. THE IMMEDIATE REVELATION OF THE TRINITY BY THE TRINITY IN THE STATE OF GLORY IS THE SUPREME GOOD AND FINAL END OF THEOLOGICAL INTERPRETATION OF SCRIPTURE

The vision of the Triune God is what the Triune God ultimately desires to give the saints (John 17:24) and what the saints ultimately desire to receive from him (Ps 27:4). Because it is the ultimate end of the Christian life, the beatific vision is the ultimate end of theological interpretation of Scripture as well.

4. B. B. Warfield, "Trinity," in *The International Standard Bible Encyclopedia*, ed. James Orr (Chicago: Howard-Severance, 1915), 5:3014.

Theological interpretation of Scripture prepares us for the vision of the Triune God by cultivating our capacities for spiritual perception and by attuning our affections to the intelligible and adorable good that the Triune God is. But theological interpretation of Scripture is more than mere preparation for this happy vision. Like the Israelite spies who tasted the grapes of Eschol before entering the Promised Land, theological interpretation of Scripture enables us to participate in this happy vision in advance by helping us perceive traces of God's Triune glory in God's good creation and by serving faith's grasp of God's Triune glory in the mediate adumbrations and attestations of that glory in the prophetic and apostolic scriptures (2 Cor 4:6).

Reading Scripture in view of its principal subject matter, the Triune God, is never therefore simply a means to understanding what Scripture can teach us about the goods of creation and salvation. To know the Triune God interpretively in holy Scripture is not merely to know his benefits. Every revelation of the Trinity in holy Scripture unveils to us our supreme good and final end—the Triune God himself. For this reason, every revelation of the Trinity in holy Scripture is an occasion for rest in the midst of our weary pilgrimage through this vale of tears, a foretaste of the river of living water that flows from the throne of God and of the Lamb (Matt 11:25–30; Rev 22:1). For this reason, every revelation of the Trinity in holy Scripture is also an occasion to rejoice in the Trinity for his own sake, and an occasion to invite others to rejoice with us as well. "Oh, magnify the Lord with me, and let us exalt his name together!" (Ps 34:3).

KEVIN J. VANHOOZER
Doers
&
Hearers
A PASTOR'S GUIDE TO MAKING DISCIPLES
THROUGH SCRIPTURE AND DOCTRINE